BREAKING THE CONNECTION

BREAKING THE CONNECTION

HOW YOUNG PEOPLE ACHIEVE DRUG-FREE LIVES

DR. ESSIE E. LEE

JULIAN MESSNER  NEW YORK
A Division of Simon & Schuster, Inc.

Copyright © 1988 by Dr. Essie E. Lee
All rights reserved
including the right of reproduction
in whole or in part in any form.
Published by Julian Messner,
A Division of Simon & Schuster Inc.,
Simon & Schuster Building,
Rockefeller Center,
1230 Avenue of the Americas,
New York, NY 10020

JULIAN MESSNER and colophon are trademarks of Simon &
Schuster Inc.

Designed by Amy Scerbo
Manufactured in the United States of America

10 9 8 7 6 5 4 3 2 1 (Lib. ed.)

10 9 8 7 6 5 4 3 2 1 (Paper ed.)

Library of Congress Cataloging-in-Publication Data

Lee, Essie E.
    Breaking the connection.

    Includes index.
    Summary: Describes the current drug epidemic and
various treatment programs. Includes case studies of
teenagers who have broken their addiction and information about different types of addictive drugs.
    1. Children—United States—Drug use—Prevention—
Juvenile literature. 2. Drug abuse—United States—
Juvenile literature. [1. Drug abuse] I. Title.
HV5824.C45L44   1988   362.2'9386   87-18586,
ISBN 0-671-63637-5 (Lib. ed.)
0-671-67059-X (Paper ed.)

PHOTO CREDITS

The following sources of photographs are gratefully acknowledged: Drug Enforcement Administration, Washington D.C., pp. 129, 136, 143; Girl Scouts of America, p. 117; Don Halasy, *New York Post,* p. 8; Frank Leonardo, *New York Post,* p. 112; Lawrence Migdale, p. 6; New Jersey Newsphotos, p. 4; *New York Post,* p. 3; *The New York Times,* pp. 104, 106, 167; Amy Seidman, p. 43; Robin Tooker, pp. 47, 54, 120.

CONTENTS

INTRODUCTION

Drug abuse is today the single greatest threat to the health and well-being of young Americans. It bears major responsibility for the high death rates of adolescents and very young adults, raising the fatal risks of violence, accidents and suicide. It closes out options for young people, diminishing opportunities for them to realize potential, pursue careers, and make productive and rewarding lives for themselves. It increases enormously the criminal involvement of the young.

Although there have been positive changes in drug use by American adolescents—fewer youngsters, for example, now smoke marijuana—overall drug use by teenagers remains extremely high, the highest of any industrialized nation. Moreover, youthful drug abuse has become more life-threatening. Use of cocaine stands at record levels, and the number of frequent users has been increasing. During the past few years, the emergence of a new form of cocaine—crack—has created a crisis of cocaine abuse among adolescents. This inexpensive and easy-to-use variety of free-base (smokable cocaine) is rapidly addicting, and young people can rarely sustain even the appearance of participating in normal school or family life once they start using crack.

Dr. Lee has described the impact of this crisis in real and chilling terms. But the young drug abusers she writes about, no matter how their drug abuse developed or what drugs they choose to use, are not much different from the many thousands of young people who have entered Phoenix House over the past 20 years. The reasons that underlie the drug abuse of young people today are those that most often underlie *all* drug abuse—anger, frustration, depression, immaturity, insecurity, and a diminished sense of self-worth.

For young drug abusers to break the connection and end profound drug dependency requires considerable strength and courage, as well as substantial help and support. It demands changes not only in behavior, but also in attitudes and feelings, sense of self and view of life. The means of treatment that will enable young people to make these changes are relatively new, for programs like Phoenix House have been in existence for little more than 20 years.

We must bear in mind that the long-term residential treatment provided by Phoenix House and programs like it is not the only answer to youthful drug abuse. Less demanding forms of treatment and intervention are also needed. So are wide-reaching drug prevention efforts, to help youngsters at risk (and that is just about all youngsters today) make positive decisions about drug use.

But we cannot depend on institutional answers alone. Treatment and intervention programs, no matter how effective, cannot reduce levels of drug abuse in a society that is not itself committed to such a goal. Nor can drug prevention programs replace parents as the first line of defense against youthful drug abuse or overcome the influence on adolescents of drug use by young adult role models.

What has most handicapped efforts to confront drug abuse in this country has not been the lack of adequate treatment resources so much as ambivalent public attitudes. We have been unwilling to use all our muscle—informal social sanctions as well as drug laws—to reduce demand for drugs. Rather, we have focused enforcement efforts on reducing supplies. We have taken a narrow view of drug prevention, one that has allowed us to tolerate what misguidedly came to be considered "social" drug use.

Today's crisis, however, is helping to shift public attitudes, and a growing intolerance for drugs is developing in the wake of increasing evidence of cocaine's devastating impact. Fewer families, friends, or employers are now willing to overlook even the occasional, discreet use of illicit drugs by young adults. Parents, who might once have ignored evidence that their kids were experimenting with marijuana, are now moving faster and confronting the problem more aggressively.

Clearly we need the resources Dr. Lee describes to deal with youthful drug abuse. Just as clearly, we need parents who are aware of the danger of drugs, certain of their own attitudes about them, and willing to take a hard-line stand against use by their children. To support parents and curb the kind of adult drug use that encourages adolescent use, we need to go beyond increased intolerance. We must be committed to the ideal of a drug-free society and be willing to use all of our muscle—formal and informal mechanisms alike—to achieve it.

Dr. Mitchell Rosenthal
Phoenix House
New York City

1
*C*RACK *I*S *I*N!

A dozen special-unit cops in unmarked cars and vans sweep down on a drug-plagued Miami neighborhood and net a dozen suspected dealers. But a short time later, it is business as usual.

In Los Angeles, dealers driving Mercedes-Benzes and BMWs and dealers wearing Fila running shoes ferry goods between buyers and their drug stashes in abandoned store-fronts and under wooden construction platforms, when a patrol car screeches to a halt and blocks off the street.

A boy of fourteen, who looks twelve, is arrested for selling two five dollar vials of crack to an undercover police officer. The sale took place on a busy street in Detroit. His supplier, age nineteen, was also arrested. Both had been in business for one week. The fourteen-year-old made $150 a day. He planned to buy shoes and clothes so he could look good in his eighth grade class. He learned about crack from his mother, a user.

On New York City's Upper West Side, plainclothes cops jump out of old Chevies and round up fourteen suspected drug dealers, some with New Jersey license plates. Other dealers and scores of lookouts with potential buyers scurry into nearby apartment house lobbies and basements like cockroaches faced with sudden bright light. During March and April 1986, the New York City Police Department's squad of 101 crack-fighting cops arrested more than 500 people, from teenagers to a seventy-one-year-old man, on felony charges related to the sale of crack, the powerful cocaine derivative that is infesting the country. The police say that as fast as they make arrests, new dealers and sellers appear. The crack trade operates like a guerrilla insurgency and makes an infuriatingly elusive target for the police. Dealers organize groups of pushers, couriers, and lookouts from the thousands of unemployed inner-city youths. The dealers enforce discipline with savage violence, change locations frequently, and alter their tactics constantly to foil undercover and narcotics agents.

"There are thousands of small-time crack dealers," federal Drug Enforcement Administration agent Robert Strong says. "There is no head of the snake to go after." Police admit that there appears to be no Mr. Big controlling the lucrative crack trade. Nor can they find evidence of involvement by traditional organized crime groups such as the Mafia. At least five million people use cocaine or crack regularly, about 25 million Americans have tried it at least once, and an additional 5,000 Americans try cocaine for the first time every day, the federal government reports. Fueled by the 500 percent increase in the amount of cocaine smuggled into this country from South America, the crack craze is spreading nationwide.

COCAINE: THE DRUG OF CHOICE

The rise in cocaine casualties in the 1980s means that for the first time, America has a widespread "hard drug" problem that affects every section of society, from the suburbs to the inner cities, and from business men and women to athletes. Cocaine and crack are equal opportunity drugs; for whites, blacks, and Hispanics, well-paid lawyers and unemployed welfare clients, cocaine is the drug of choice.

In June 1986, a five-year study published by Johns Hopkins Medical Institution claimed that one out of every twenty individuals who use cocaine reports psychological or physical prob-

Marijuana is still popular but bulky to transport and easy for customs officers to spot.

Two hundred and seventy-five kilos of cocaine and $900,000 were confiscated by police in a raid in Leonia, New Jersey.

lems related to the drug. It was the first study of cocaine use in a general population. James C. Anthony and his colleagues followed 15,000 adults in Baltimore, St. Louis, New Haven, and Durham. There were 3,045 cocaine users in the group. Most had used it five times or less, but about 15 percent became daily users. A problem many users reported was "tolerance"— meaning that the user needs to take increasingly larger amounts to achieve the same effect. Many had trouble with school, jobs, and personal relations. Social or job problems were reported by 2 percent of users in Baltimore, 9 percent in St. Louis, and 15 percent in Durham. Tolerance was reported to be a problem by 1 percent in Baltimore, 2 percent in St. Louis, and 3 percent in Durham.

Cocaine is also the drug of choice of drug traffickers. They consider it the near-perfect illegal drug. Marijuana is bulky; multimillion dollar loads must be moved in large slow-moving cargo ships that are easy to intercept. Heroin, though compact and profitable, appeals to far fewer people, and its use is unlikely to spread much beyond the estimated half a million hard core users counted in 1986. "Heroin was always in the slums, somebody abusing himself who was willing to put a needle into his body," Representative Lynn M. Martin says. She is an Illinois Republican who is active on drug committees.

But cocaine is compact, popular, and profitable. An attaché case full of the drug can bring $500,000 at wholesale, and retail prices can be extraordinarily profitable. Law enforcement agencies report that although the wholesale price of the drug has fallen from about $23,000 a pound four years ago to as little as $7,300 in some parts of the country today, the retail price has barely changed. Individual users in 1987 still pay about eighty to one hundred dollars for one gram, or 0.03 ounces.

KIDS AND COCAINE

Crack is a purified form of cocaine that comes in pellet form and is smoked rather than snorted. Dealers make crack by mixing cocaine with common baking soda, creating a paste that

A teenager sniffs cocaine on a theater stairway.

is usually at least 75 percent cocaine. The paste hardens and is cut into chips that resemble soap or whitish gravel. A small piece, sometimes called a "quarter rock," produces a high lasting twenty to thirty minutes. It is smoked in water pipes, empty soda or fruit juice cans, or clay pipes.

Crack is creating social havoc in the poor sections of Los Angeles, New York, Miami, Chicago, and other large cities, and it is rapidly spreading into the suburbs on both coasts. Its cheapness and easy availability are probably major reasons that cocaine abuse among the young is on the rise, although national surveys do not distinguish between cocaine in its usual form and crack.

"Right now, we don't know the answer," says Edgar Adams, epidemiologist and statistician at the National Institute on Drug Abuse. "Is crack responsible for the increase [in drug abuse], or is the increase responsible for crack? We do know that cocaine use has gone up among high-school seniors, and we have been hearing about crack for eight months or so. I think it's entirely feasible that as the price has gone down you've had more people able to try it." Adams believes that crack is a drug dealer's dream. It is easy to prepare, easy to use, easy to hide— and a single dose sells for as little as ten to fifteen dollars in most places. Dr. Arnold Washton, of Fair Oaks Hospital in Summit, New Jersey, says, "It's like fast food. It's a quick-sale product. Because it transforms the occasional cocaine user into an addictive user, it is much more likely to yield a repeat customer."

Although the dealer may be an adult, crack is usually peddled by juveniles. This is largely because in most states, teenagers do not normally face heavy penalties when arrested. Crowded jails, few judges, and plea bargaining also help keep youths out of jail.

The findings of the twelfth annual national survey of 130 high schools by the University of Michigan's Institute for Social Research show that young people are turning away from illegal drugs—with one exception: cocaine and its derivatives. The study's findings, made public in February 1987, found that

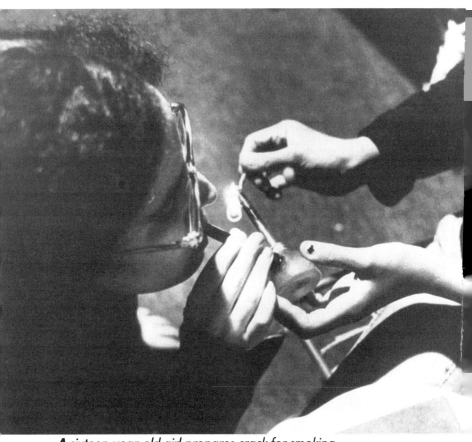

A sixteen-year-old girl prepares crack for smoking.

although the proportion of high school students using cocaine has not changed greatly since 1980, the number of frequent users and students who cannot stop using the drug has increased significantly since 1983. Experts link the increase in the frequent users to the rise in the smoking of cocaine, including the smoking of the potent crack.

Of the 15,200 students interviewed, 16.9 percent said they had tried cocaine at least once, 12.7 percent had used it in the past year, and 6.2 percent had taken it in the last 30 days.

The group of daily cocaine users doubled between 1983 and 1986, from 0.2 to 0.4 percent of the seniors, and the students who said they had at some time been unable to stop rose from 0.4 percent in 1983 to 0.8 percent in 1986. This represents a total of 25,000 addicted students nationwide, the study said.

The proportion of students who said they had smoked—rather than simply inhaled—cocaine in the last year rose from 2.5 percent in 1983 to 6 percent in 1986. In its first survey of crack use, the study found 4.1 percent of the seniors last year had smoked cocaine in this form. "Considering how dangerous [crack is], even 4 percent is a very disturbing figure," said Dr. Lloyd Johnson, project director at the institute.

Measured against the powerful temptation that cocaine offers, society's attempts to deter young people from drug use seem mostly ineffectual. Many drug-abuse experts quietly concede that in-school drug prevention programs, necessary though they may be, have largely failed to reach their teenage audience. There is still widespread disagreement about the root causes of drug abuse and equally little consensus on the best tactics for prevention.

Law enforcement, similarly, has had some impact in deterring young users but not nearly enough. In the bleak view of many drug experts, drug use will persist among teenagers in America as long as adult Americans condone it—and adult America, they say, tacitly accepts drugs in many forms, cocaine included.

HOW COCAINE WORKS

Now, after a decade of research, professionals know much more about the peculiarities of the drug and the ways it interacts with and alters various cells, organs, and bodily systems in laboratory animals and in humans. Clinicians using case histories from doctors' offices, emergency rooms, and morgues have put together a picture of what moderate to heavy use of cocaine does to someone over a period of months or years. These researchers and pharmacologists have recently begun to try to bring the public image of cocaine into line with scientific reality.

Cocaine, they say, is one of the most dangerous drugs in the underground market. It's physically debilitating, whether you snort it, swallow it, inject it, or smoke it. A constant running nose is the least of its drawbacks. Those who frequently snort substantial amounts of the drug can develop chronic sore throats, inflamed sinuses, hoarseness, and sometimes even holes in the cartilage of the nose. For those who inject cocaine, hepatitis from dirty needles is always possible. Freebasers may destroy the ability of living cells to process gases, leaving the person with a constant cough and often shortness of breath.

There is also evidence that cocaine can worsen pre-existing weaknesses of the heart, as well as initiate full-blown heart attacks. If the user has heart disease, the rapid pulse and pounding heart that accompany the high can degenerate into heart failure and death. Epidemiologist Dr. Diane Sauter says some of the patients she sees at Bellevue Hospital's Emergency Department in New York "are brought to emergency rooms in cardiac arrest (no heart beat) or they come in the day after using crack complaining of chest pains. Doctors haven't really discovered if these are the result of the hot gases acting on the lungs or upper airways. Some people take more cocaine than they have ever used. Others apprehended, and about to be arrested, swallow the evidence, resulting in cocaine poisoning with palpitations and even seizures."

At Harlem Hospital, also in New York City, Dr. Reynold

Trowers, chief of Emergency Services, is overwhelmed with the increase of cases being brought to the hospital. "We're getting China white, black tar—two heroin synthetics—crack, cocaine, and spacebase, which is crack laced with PCP (phencyclidine, known on the street as "angel dust"). They come in with chest pains, shaking-all-over paranoia, delusional, psychotic, and violent behavior. An increasing number are younger than thirty years old." A newspaper reporter tells of a screaming and moaning female patient who came in with PCP overdose:

> Around the hysterical woman's bed they are tying her legs. . . . She is making a face as if she were trying to blow her brains out of her mouth. She has no shoes on, and her feet look as though she has been barefoot for a while. There are cuts on the top of her feet and worn polish on her toenails. Her eyebrows are freshly arched. Her fingernails are manicured. She refuses to say what she's taken. "Take a deep breath and hold it, don't breathe," says a resident as Dr. Trowers sticks a long needle in a vein in her neck.

According to Dr. Trowers, 30 to 40 percent of the emergency patients at Harlem Hospital have drug or alcohol problems.

WHY CRACK IS SO ADDICTIVE

Scientists say that crack alters brain chemistry and moods in the same way as cocaine powder. But it does so more rapidly and more intensely, producing not only a higher "high" but also a deeper "crash" that leaves the user desperate for more. Researchers are zeroing in on exactly how cocaine and its derivatives produce euphoria and the depression and craving that follow. The drug interferes with the normal functioning of neurotransmitters, chemicals that activate nerves in an area of the brain associated with pleasurable feelings, according to Dr.

Roger M. Brown, chief of Neuroscience at the National Institute on Drug Abuse.

In human beings, nerve endings are separated by tiny gaps known as synapses. When a message, in the form of an electrical impulse, reaches a nerve ending, it stimulates the release of a neurotransmitter that crosses the gap, carrying the message to the receiving nerve. Their job done, some of the transmitters are broken down, and the rest are sucked back into the first nerve.

Cocaine blocks this "sucking back" or retrieval process for three neurotransmitters that are involved in the regulation of mood and motor function in the body. "Once the transmitter is released, there has to be a way of inactivating it," says Dr. Brown. "Otherwise the signal pounds away." With inactivation hampered by cocaine, then, the normal effect of the chemicals is multiplied.

Erik Eckholm wrote in the *New York Times* of August 17, 1986,

> According to current theory, repeated doses of cocaine produce a temporary shortage of the transmitters; as their reabsorption for later use is blocked, the body degrades them faster than it manufactures new chemicals. Soon, not enough transmitters are present even to maintain a normal mood, resulting in depression, anxiety and a hunger for more cocaine to enhance the effectiveness of the depleted supply. Heavy prolonged cocaine use may eventually deplete the transmitter so totally that euphoria is unattainable and depression cannot be forestalled. This probably accounts for the "binge and crash" pattern seen in many addicts, experts theorize.

All of these effects are accentuated with crack, according to Eckholm. Crack comes in concentrated pellets. When inhaled as smoke into the lungs, the drug shoots through the blood-stream much more quickly than it does when the powder form is snorted. The letdown comes quickly too. Dr. Charles R. Schuster, director of the National Institute on Drug Abuse, says that the acceleration of the process itself helps boost crack's appeal. "The faster the change, the greater the euphoria," he believes.

PSYCHOLOGICAL STATES IN THE COCAINE USER

For heavy cocaine users, it is possible to swing through four distinct psychological states after a binge or spree. The first state is the euphoric high that usually lasts ten to thirty minutes and ends with depression, hallucination, and psychosis. One long-term user describes it like this, "Not only is your energy gone, but your whole head changes too. Good feelings start to fade away and eventually depression sets in."

After months of regular binging, the user will become "coked out." Depression becomes chronic, the user begins hallucinating, and signs of psychosis (complete mental de-rangement) appear. Psychosis is preceded by a short temper, suspicion, and increased irritability. Lisa Benson, public infor-mation representative at Fair Oaks Hospital in Summit, New Jersey, says that in a survey of 500 calls to their telephone hotline, researchers found that half reported symptoms of this nature. Eighty-three percent of the group, all of whom took cocaine almost daily, told interviewers they felt habitually de-pressed or anxious. At least half said they had difficulty concen-trating or remembering things, were uninterested in sex, and sometimes had panic attacks. With continuous and increased use of cocaine, symptoms in the user become more pro-nounced.

DEATH AND SUDDEN DEATH

For the weekend or casual cocaine user who believes that he or she will never go beyond euphoria, the most frightening news is that cocaine can kill suddenly. Taken in any form and any dose over 60 milligrams, cocaine can kill. Dr. Louis L. Cregler, assistant chief of medicine at the Bronx Veterans Administration Medical Center in New York, says that deaths have been reported after ingestion by any method. Most such deaths are attributed to cocaine intoxication, leading to convulsions, respiratory failure, and cardiac arrhythmias (irregular heartbeats) minutes to hours after administration. Much information on this process is so new that it hasn't found its way into the medical literature or standard textbooks.

"The number of cocaine related deaths has risen rapidly since 1983, reaching the highest level ever recorded," reports Dr. Blanche Frank, chief of epidemiology for New York State's Division of Substance Abuse Services. Cocaine triggers heart attacks, a fact dramatized by the deaths of two star athletes— Len Bias, talented University of Maryland forward and first draft choice of the Boston Celtics, and Don Rogers, defensive back of the Cleveland Browns. The United States Public Health Services report that the number of cocaine-caused deaths tripled in five years, to 563 in 1985. The agency estimates that there will be 13,000 cocaine-caused emergency room cases in 1987.

In New York City, the number of cocaine-related deaths jumped from 7 in 1983 to 137 in 1985. Cocaine abuse is blamed for an ever-increasing proportion of narcotic deaths. In 1985, only 1 percent of all local narcotic deaths was linked to cocaine, compared with 16 percent in 1984 and 20.4 percent in 1985.

The only good news about cocaine is that users are suddenly scared. The sudden deaths of the two athletes have resulted in great increases—up to 60 percent—in calls to New York State's cocaine hot line. Most callers want the newest information on crack.

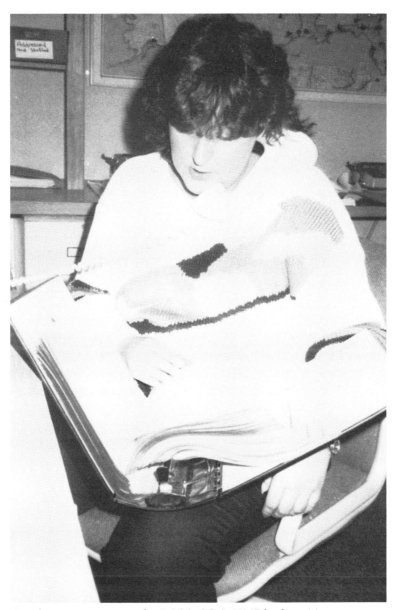

A volunteer answering the 1-800-COC-AINE hotline. More than fifty referrals are made daily.

CRACK, VIOLENCE AND MURDER

In New York City, police report that the crack epidemic has been responsible for a sharp increase in crime. Examples of serious crime related to drug abuse make grim reading.

- A two-year-old boy was beaten to death by his 23-year-old mother's boyfriend. Arguments about money needed for food instead of crack led to the killing.

- A four-year-old girl was thrown from the window of her eighteenth floor apartment by her addicted uncle who fifteen minutes earlier had smoked crack.

- A Transit Authority maintenance worker allegedly "desperate for crack" was arrested and charged with stabbing to death a subway token clerk in a robbery to support his habit.

- Three suspects were arraigned on charges of sexually abusing and beating a twenty-one-year-old man, because he lost thirty-five dollars the men gave him to buy crack.

- A teenager was indicted on murder and arson charges for allegedly setting his home on fire when his mother refused to give him money to buy crack. She died of a heart attack during the incident.

- A fifty-nine-year-old man was arrested for shooting his employer and co-worker when caught removing money from the cash register. He claimed he needed the money for crack.

- A sixteen-year-old walked into a police precinct and announced that he killed his mother during a quarrel over his use of crack.

- A twenty-four-year-old mother was stabbed to death while her four-year-old daughter screamed in terror. The attacker had smoked crack ten minutes earlier.

- An eighty-two-year-old woman was slain by a young purse snatcher, who needed cash to support his crack habit.

"There is no question there is a close correlation between the recent increase we've experienced in violent crime and the increase . . . in the use of drugs," says Deputy Chief Francis C. Hall, commander of the New York City Police Department's narcotics division.

In two federally financed studies, one of which was conducted in 1984 and the other in 1986, a total of more than 5,000 men who were arrested and detained in central booking in Manhattan were asked to submit urine samples voluntarily for drug testing. In both studies, about 85 percent of those who were asked to submit a sample did so. Of those who agreed to be tested, 78 percent tested positive for cocaine use in the fall of 1986, compared with only 42 percent in 1984. The use of other drugs was not found to have increased in the same period.

This increase in cocaine use was found for all age levels, but was especially high for men between 16 and 25 years old. In the 16- to 20-year-old group, 28 percent of those tested showed cocaine use in 1984. By the fall of 1986, that number had risen to 71 percent. In the 21- to 25-year-old category, the rise was from 43 percent using cocaine in 1984 to 91 percent in 1986. These results were so striking that similar Drug Use Forcasting Systems are to be set up in ten other cities before the end of 1987.

FOR WOMEN: THE CHAMPAGNE OF DRUGS

At a meeting of the President's Commission on Organized Crime held on November 29, 1984, in Washington, D.C., Dr. Arnold Washton gave testimony regarding women's use of cocaine. The doctor is a drug researcher at Regent Hospital in New York City and research director of the cocaine hot line at Fair Oaks Hospital, Summit, New Jersey. He testified that of the nearly 500,000 calls the line received in 1983, one-third were from women. In 1984, almost half the callers had been women. "Cocaine use among women had jumped in the last year as the price has plummeted, and some young men are even sending it to their girlfriends instead of candy or flowers," said Dr. Washton.

The cocaine-abusing woman may be anyone from a housewife or a high school student to a high-powered executive. Female addicts appear less likely to seek treatment. Some professionals feel this is because society rejects women with this kind of addiction. Many don't feel that they can be cured, so they don't even seek help.

Researchers see cocaine as having an overpowering appeal to women. An administrator at the New York Stuyvesant Square chemical dependency program says, "You can put it in a little tube and carry it around in your cosmetic bag. Women might not feel comfortable drinking in a bar for hours, but cocaine is a nice, neat drug—for women who want to deceive themselves."

The ideal female is thin, and coke has a reputation as an appetite suppressant, according to Dr. Josette Mondanaro, a former head of drug abuse clinics in California. In fact, about 25 percent of bulimics—sufferers of the binge/purge syndrome—are drug users. The 1980s ideal woman is also a "supermom." She brings money into the family by day and is the perfect lover at night. Cocaine has the reputation of providing boundless energy. But at the same time, as Dr. Mondanaro says, "We still live in a society that denigrates women—and most women suffer from low self-esteem. And now along comes a drug that bolsters self-esteem and provides a momentary sense of accomplishment. Instead of being depressed, a woman can be euphoric."

Dr. Jeffrey Rosecan, director of the Cocaine Abuse Treatment Program at Columbia Presbyterian Medical Center in New York, sees female patients who in the initial stages of their addiction feel confident, flirtatious, outgoing, thin, sensual, and desirable. "You can see how women get sucked into it," says Jane Velez, president of the drug treatment program Project Return. "You walk into a party, and you feel a little uncomfortable. A lot of people are snorting, so you do a line (sniff cocaine) yourself. And suddenly you feel great. The next day you get up, and unlike with alcohol you don't feel so bad. You remember how witty you were. And a week later, in the same situation, you go and do it again."

Ironically, although cocaine can make women feel sexy and competent, it can also serve as the basis for an oppressive relationship. More than 85 percent of the female callers to the 1-800 COC-AINE hot line had been introduced to cocaine by men. Sixty-five percent continued to get cocaine as gifts or payment for sexual favors. "Often the relationship gets cemented by cocaine, and the women become completely dependent," says Dr. Margaret Eaton, consultant psychologist at the Out-Patient Recovery Center at Regent Hospital in New York. "The man is keeping them supplied or not supplied; he is in control, and they'll accommodate themselves to whatever he wants."

At Phoenix House Foundation in Manhatten, Director Naomi Kline-McDermott, M.S.W., called just Naomi by almost everyone, confirms these professionals' findings. "We're seeing an increase in women who are using crack. More disturbing is learning about the degrading things women are doing to get drugs." Naomi lists among them prostitution and pornographic films, and bizarre sex acts that can include physical pain. "In the old days," Naomi says, "if you asked a woman how she supported her habit, she would say 'I turn tricks.' But today, the women aren't even aware that what they're doing is prostitution at its worst." At Phoenix House, Naomi gives women priority. "Women are usually second-class citizens to begin with, so we give them more attention, more services, and more time." Young female teenagers who live in crack houses bring additional problems. Many give themselves to dealers, suppliers, and buyers in return for crack. "When they finally seek help, these kids are so confused. They can't even understand that their benefactors have been their greatest enemies," says Naomi.

BABIES OF CRACK USERS

An unexpected and unfortunate side effect of the crack invasion is its effect on an increasing number of babies born to crack-addicted mothers. Because many of the parents are unable to care for their newborns and foster-care parents are fearful of any child born of addicted parents, many of these babies become boarders in municipal hospitals where they may remain for weeks or months. "When foster-care families hear there was use of crack by the parents, it raises additional concerns," says Eric Brettschneider, deputy administrator in charge of special services for children at New York City's Human Resources Administration. "Rationally or irrationally, they become concerned about AIDS (acquired immune deficiency syndrome) and the additional responsibility of caring for a child who may be medically frail." Mr. Brettschneider estimates that several hundred infants will wait for placement in hospitals over the next several months.

At Kings County Hospital, professor of pediatrics Dr. Leonard Glass said the increase in crack-using mothers had led to a steady rise in premature births and infants with low birthweights. Between one-third and one-half of the infants of crack users have cocaine in their urine or show signs of neurological disorders, including irritability, tremors, muscle rigidity, and stiffness. In contrast to the conditions of babies of heroin addicts, the symptoms of withdrawal are generally milder and subside in two or four days, Dr. Glass says.

Boarder babies are straining already limited resources at other city hospitals. With reduced budgets, the hospitals cannot hire the additional nurses needed for the tasks of feeding and substituting for a mother figure. At Lincoln Hospital the 15 boarders need someone to talk to them, to hold them, and to provide a maternal link. Kings County's nursery has up to 29 boarders who are limiting space available for admission of ill babies.

One solution to the problem is to ask for volunteers to "mother" these infants. Dozens of women and men responded to New York City Mayor Edward Koch's request for volunteers, made in February 1987. These adult volunteers, many parents themselves, are screened for characteristics which make them suitable for this sensitive responsibility.

Child care agencies cite increases in reports of child abuse that are related to increases in crack use. "We see cases where children are left alone without supervision when parents go out to get drugs," Brettschneider reports. "A parent who becomes overwhelmed with drug needs and loses sight of feeding the child just leaves the house." The number of children of crack-using parents needing foster care will continue to climb, predicts Philip Coltoff, executive director of the Childrens Aid Society, one of the largest providers of foster homes in New York City.

A possible legal precedent is being set in Florida. Florida officials are considering seeking what may be the nation's first criminal prenatal child abuse charges against a drug-using mother whose baby was born with a cocaine addiction. "Our position is that the child was abused before it was born," said State Attorney Bruce Colton. "The mother was using cocaine during the entire course of the pregnancy, and that is as much an abuse as if she had harmed the child in some way after it was born."

Assistant State Attorney David Morgan said criminal charges would have to be brought under the child abuse law, but Florida does not specifically address prenatal abuse. So attorneys are investigating how to proceed. The baby, who is on medicine to wean her of cocaine addiction, now weights nearly 5 pounds and would not need hospitalization if placed with someone trained to give proper care, the prosecutor added. In August 1986, the baby was still receiving medical care. The mother is a cocaine user, a prostitute, and has no home address.

CRACK AND THE MIDDLE CLASS

"After fifteen years and a lot of hard work, I finally got promoted," says a full professor at a noted southern university. "I'd never even smoked a cigarette, so I was totally unprepared for any kind of drug use. But at a party, a colleague gave me some crack." Several others at the party were smoking from glass bowls and, to the novice, it looked intriguing. "I was told that it was a dynamite form of cocaine." He remembers many of his fellow workers using cocaine down through the years, and they seemed to function without difficulty.

"Within three months, the stuff controlled my life," the professor says. It is easy to be an addict of any kind in a college setting. Working hours are irregular, and classes may be scheduled for mornings, afternoons, or evenings. It is a short work week too. "You can come in, teach, and go home. Most of my work could be done off-campus, like the reading, the writing, and committee work."

The $57,000 a year habit of the professor's cost up to $450 a week, but financially he was in no danger. Income from research grants, publications, presentations, and consultations made up any deficit. But physically, the professor paid a high price. He lacked energy and canceled his twice-a-week tennis game with his best friend. He was too tired to jog or even take his daily stroll. His appetite was jaded. A weight loss of 25 pounds caused his clothes to hang unattractively. Twice in one month, the professor didn't meet with his classes. He was eventually summoned to the department chairman's office to explain himself.

Similar stories are being told by a growing number of people who have entered drug treatment programs for crack addiction in recent months. It illustrates an aspect of the crack epidemic that has gone unnoticed, drug experts say.

Although little demographic data have been collected, agency reports in 1986 indicate that many addicts are people with jobs that pay well and that the majority are adults, not teenagers.

According to administrators of treatment centers like Odyssey House's Ben Walker, Jr., many of the college-educated and professional people who smoke crack have snorted cocaine on occasion for years. And for years, they have dismissed warnings about this drug as exaggerated.

AFFLUENT SUBURBS TOO

As crack use spreads through cities and suburbs, a growing number of middle-class casual drug users are surprised to find themselves suffering a severe crack addiction. Dr. Jules P. is one. Son of a prominent surgeon, he is a highly successful internist with a lucrative practice in Dallas, Texas. Dr. P. owns an expensive twelve-room suburban home, a condominium in town, a Jamaica retreat, and a Lear jet with seating for ten. With his three children tucked safely away in boarding schools, Dr. P. and his wife are free to enjoy the good life.

Like many of his lawyer, banker, and executive-type friends, Dr. P. has been a casual user of cocaine since his undergraduate days. He says that snorting cocaine was one of the things to do at long weekend parties and evenings at the country club. Then came crack, which changed everyone's life-style. "The first time that I tried it was like being shot out of a cannon at one hundred miles an hour. The reaction was that fast and excruciatingly pleasurable. Each time I take it, I know that nothing will stop me from doing it again within 4 to 6 hours." Dr. P. is a well-heeled junkie now in treatment in New York City.

Despite media reports that relate crack use to teenagers, the poor, and those living in inner-city areas, evidence gathered in several studies shows that crack has made substantial inroads among the professional and upper middle class adults who used powdered cocaine in the past. Unlike teenagers who can be seen selling crack and smoking openly in the poorer neighborhoods of large cities, professionals say affluent crack users are less public in their habits and are less likely to be noticed. For example, employees of the street research unit of New York's State Division of Substance Abuse Services frequently visit spots where street dealers sell amounts of cocaine and marijuana to workers from office buildings in the Wall Street,

Liberty Plaza, and Battery Park areas of New York's financial district. Drug runners and dealers hawk crack, or "jumbo,"as it is sometimes called. Also for sale are "V"s and "E"s, code letters for Valium and Elavil, prescription tranquilizers and antidepressants. Both are used with crack to blunt or slow down sudden, depressive plunges after the highs. Drugs are passed through a quick handshake and a smile that easily passes as a casual, friendly greeting.

Stories of addicted computer programmers, systems analysts, stock brokers, and investment bankers abound in this revered world of high finance. Many use crack three or four times within 12 hours. Others use it less frequently, but it is always secretive. Traffic to restrooms, lounges, and basement garages is excessive as the addicted take their crack breaks. At some firms, production is down while employee absenteeism is up. The average user can spend up to $400 a day supporting a habit.

THE FUTURE OF COCAINE IN AMERICA

Years of study with other narcotics has shown that when the public perception of a drug's dangers increases, use of the substance declines. This was true for marijuana: Government surveys showed that in 1978, as more people began to believe marijuana was harmful, the number using the drug began to drop.

Dr. Donald McDonald, White House special assistant for drug abuse policy, claims that this was true for LSD in the 1970s and PCP and quaaludes in the 1980s, as well as for other drugs at other times. But he sees a different trend in cocaine use, partly because of the strength of the drug's addictive effect. "Cocaine stimulates parts of the brain that increase the user's desire for the drug. The National Institute on Drug Abuse calls cocaine the most powerful psychological reinforcer of any of the illicit drugs, creating a profound dependency," he says.

For late 1986, charts depicting trends in cocaine use alongside the evolving public perception of the drug's danger show two simultaneously climbing lines. "Part of the difficulty lies in the fact that now the United States has yuppies instead of hippies. And cocaine is associated with their, the yuppies', values—success, mastery, and control. It's a self-marketing product," concludes Dr. Washton, of Fair Oaks Hospital. And, at least for now, there is little sign that America's cocaine addiction is fading.

2
THIS IS THE
LAST STOP

The 74th Street lobby was deserted. Things appeared very quiet. It was July and hot. Perhaps drugs had taken a holiday. But when the elevator door opened at the basement level, it was quite evident that drugs were alive and well. The reception area of this treatment facility was crowded. Several young people squatted on the floor. Their clothes were typical of the light costumes kids fashion out of long skirts, big shirts, miniskirts, short shorts, halters, T-shirts, saw-tooth edged jeans, ballet slippers, and sneakers. Parents with worry lines creasing their tired faces sit with their teenage children. A tall, heavyset girl sits bent over with her long black hair cascading toward the floor. A perspiring youth propped up in a corner removes his red "I Luv New York" T-shirt and rolls it into a pillow; and a middle-aged woman lies stretched out on the floor between the two rows of occupied chairs. Her narrow skirt is tucked demurely between long, thin legs.

This is the admission area of Phoenix House Foundation. The treatment agency has enjoyed a reputation for twenty years as one of the most prominent rehabilitation facilities in the world. With a staff of more than three hundred operating ten programs in New York and California, Phoenix House provides services to more than fifteen thousand people each year. Like

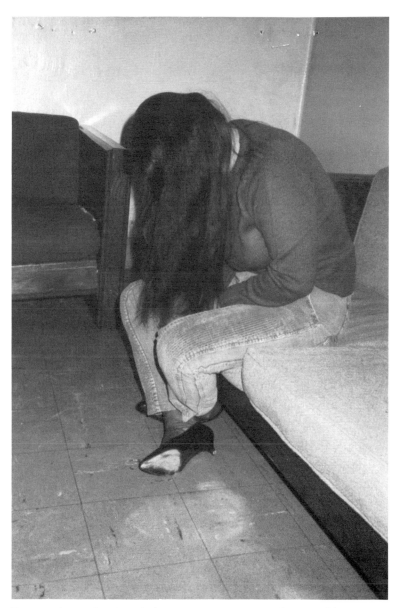

Despondent, afraid and alone, a teenager waits for possible admission to treatment at Phoenix House.

A counselor leading a group therapy session for Phoenix House.

other drug treatment facilities in the greater New York area, Phoenix House is responding to the crack epidemic.

THERE'S A WAR GOING ON OUT THERE

For the first time, agencies are struggling to avoid turning away clients as more people become addicted to crack. From the wealthiest suburbs of Westchester and Long Island counties, Connecticut and New Jersey, to the poor sections of the Bronx and Bedford Stuyvesant in New York City, drug experts say the growth of crack has been so great that it is fast outpacing the ability of treatment and rehabilitation programs to cope with the problem.

At Phoenix House, Director Naomi Kline-McDermott and her efficient staff are working overtime to avoid waiting lists of addicts who have come forward pleading for help. "This is the last stop or they wouldn't be here," Naomi says. "The war has spread dramatically in the first six months of 1986, particularly among adolescents. How can we turn them back to the war out there?" she asks, not expecting a response. "Not all will be admitted," says the director, referring to the crowded reception area, "because what we really do is diagnose and assess the appropriateness for treatment." Years ago, professionals believed that everyone should be helped. "We were not selective and tried to help people, because we decided that they needed help." But that philosophy changed as the drug-using population grew larger and the experts became more scientific, using a team approach in screening and creating protocols for admission. Medical professionals also realized that clients had to assume some responsibility in their treatment programs. Therapy is designed to meet individual needs and the facility is not appropriate for everyone who appears at the door.

CAN YOU HELP ME?

The tall, thin, perspiring young man had been observed by a staff member as he waited in the reception area. Although all clients are considered to be "in crisis" here, an alert counselor recognized symptoms and signs in this patient that required hospitalization. These were lethargy, a pale, sweating face, the "shakes" and an uneasy gait. His long, thin arms hung loosely out of a short-sleeved shirt. Both arms were heavily tattooed with Harley-Davidson motorcycle insignia. His name was Phil and he had not eaten in several days. As Naomi questioned him, he slumped downward in the chair. Phil looked extremely sick, with his slurred speech and half-opened eyes. He spoke of trying to kill himself four times within the last six months. His sleeping had been sporadic and he was limp from sheer exhaustion. In an almost inaudible voice, Phil told of smoking an unknown quantity of angel dust over the last twelve hours. When hospitalization was suggested, he began to cry. "Please not that," he begged with large tears sliding down his unshaven face. "My stomach was pumped out the last time and I can't take it again," Phil pleaded. Naomi waited patiently for Phil to gain control, before she explained the need to be drug-free before any kind of treatment could be started. For now, hospitalization was a must. Phil asked for John Sheehan, Naomi's deputy assistant. Through the grapevine, Phil had learned that John was a "great guy." John was summoned and greeted Phil warmly.

Both Naomi and John reassured Phil that he would be better off in a hospital. Because he was heavily sedated, any assessment at that time would have been worthless. After his body was drug-free, a counselor would be available for discussion. John's sensitive responses convinced Phil, and supported by John's strong arms, both went out to seek a cab. Naomi telephoned her contact at the hospital who would prepare for Phil's admission.

PLEASE TELEPHONE FIRST

Although everyone who comes to Phoenix House is considered by the counseling staff to be in dire distress, those who are suicidal, psychotic, and having anxiety attacks require immediate attention. But, like Phil, they are referred elsewhere for appropriate medical care.

A telephone screening system that clarifies the type of services available can save valuable time in assessing drug users seeking treatment. Callers are told that certain conditions preclude admission. These can include current hospitalization, involvement with the police, being on medication for a serious ailment, and a current legal situation, like a hearing or a trial that will be time-consuming. A parent may make an appointment for a child, but although a friend, relative, or neighbor may call seeking help for someone, adults must make their own appointments. When friends or relatives call, some advice and an explanation of available services is given. The caller may be invited to visit the facility too, if further help is needed.

Telephoning ahead lets Phoenix House begin the task of gathering information about the potential client and enables staff to set aside sufficient time for a thorough screening interview. It also provides time for the staff to explain what is and what is not possible in the way of services. Counselors take notes and compare them later with the information given at the interview conducted in person. "At times," says Naomi, "it may be too painful [for the client] to disclose the real reason for telephoning. So a more acceptable or common reason will be given over the telephone." An experienced counselor will guide the client to identifying a more valid reason for coming to Phoenix House.

THE SCREENING INTERVIEW

The client is told to come to his or her appointment well rested and drug-free. This includes not taking any alcohol or tobacco. Obviously, it would be impossible to interview an intoxicated person, and any medication may hide a psychotic disorder. Information about the client is collected in a friendly, informal manner. The counselor hopes to build an "identity" that includes medical history, educational background, work history, family structure, psychiatric history if any, previous hospitalizations, and other relevant information. Honesty is required of the client and full disclosure is important, because a treatment program is designed based on these data; false statements result in inappropriate planning and placement. During the rather lengthy interview, the counselor will observe the client's body language, degree of his or her interest, consistency of eye contact, and the amount and quality of the client's input.

The counselor will look for signs of underlying problems to which others are related. The client may request special hours or days or show unusual restlessness. The counselor must be alert to the possibility that he or she is receiving kidney dialysis several times a week or is facing a pending prison sentence or needs detoxification.

Work history is very important, since it indicates a level of functioning in the client. Phoenix House has several treatment programs, and some require stability with a long and consistent work history. Means of support is another indication of functioning. For instance, if a young person is collecting government supplements or disability checks, he or she may have an emotional or physical problem that prevents employment.

Educational level, especially in the young, tells the counselor a lot about the client. Will he or she need help with basic reading and writing skills? Does he or she have a problem with authority figures, accepting criticism, or relating to people? At times, the answers show that a person can be functional in school but not in the real world.

Youngsters not yet cighteen must be accompanied by a parent. Not only is it illegal to question the youngster, but an adult's signature is required for consent to treatment and release of any personal information. "Ideally, parents should accompany anyone under twenty-one, but Phoenix House will not turn away an eighteen-year-old who cannot get his or her parent's cooperation." Naomi finds that most parents are at the end of their rope. "They've tried everything. And once they see the kid trying to do something positive on his or her own, they are happy to help." When counselors work with youngsters in continuing sessions, parents are required to attend four orientation meetings. The director explains: "Parents learn about our philosophy, how and why it works, and the rules and regulations. Staff members build an alliance with parents. If a kid wants to leave, parents are now our partners rather than our enemies." She adds, "And then too, it gives us a chance to learn about possible family supports and nonsupports which influence the youngster's recovery."

*G*ETTING TO KNOW YOU

An intensive interview follows the screening stage. This is the time when facts are assessed and decisions are made regarding placement in one of Phoenix House's several drug treatment programs. What does it take? Naomi's staff looks for a fairly healthy individual who is free of acute disease, capable of self-care, not in need of outside medical treatment, able to talk and physically fit, and able to engage in a program. The client's drug history is scrutinized carefully, along with any possibilities of suicidal tendencies. Former psychiatric admissions, if any, are explored in depth, as well as history of violent behavior, seizures, blackouts, or psychopathic episodes.

Dependent upon the findings and degree of client cooperation, this session can be lengthy. A careful evaluation of the completed forms and counselor's assessment by supervisory staff determines the type of program best suited for the client's needs. Programs at Phoenix House are designed for two age groups—adolescents and adults.

*H*ELPING KIDS

IMPACT (Intervention Moves Parents and Children Together) is an after-school program designed to help families stop early drug use by adolescents. Youngsters attend sessions with others of their own age at least three times a week, while family involvement starts with six weeks of parent education seminars, and continues with therapy involving several family groups. Youth assigned to the program are attending school and able to continue to do so. There is also a stable family environment at home with parents willing to be involved. The young person may be an occasional truant and cut classes and commit minor offenses at school. But there is enough control to manage the problem outside of an institution.

"Step One School" is a collaborative effort of Phoenix House and the New York City Board of Education. This is a day program that helps teenagers between the ages of twelve and eighteen. Kids in this program may have committed minor offenses. Some leave home every morning intent on going to school, but never make it; others frequently break curfew at home. There may be very minor law violations, but nothing serious.

Parental participation in this program is mandatory. Without it, Phoenix House will not enroll the youngster. It is for kids who need supervision. They spend eight hours, five days a week, at the facility, including the summer months. Most remain in the program for a year with the goal of going back into a full school program. In assessment, the staff looks for a moderate degree of functioning at home, at school, and with peers.

DOING TWENTY-FOUR/SEVEN

Twenty-four hours a day, seven days a week means residential treatment. Although confined, many kids admitted to this program grow to love the beautiful country setting of rolling, green hills of New York or California, where they live in special treatment centers. Naomi says, "Kids are treated differently from adults. And they should be, since their job is not to be an adult but to be a kid." Youngsters sixteen and older are placed in a therapeutic community designed especially for them. There is a two-week induction course before the youngsters arrive at

Naomi in her office ready to meet with troubled young people.

either Shrub Oak, New York, or Santa Ana, California. During this period, they see a physician and a psychiatrist. When they arrive, they begin Phase One, a two-month period of orientation to Phoenix House's philosophy and the demands of a new life-style. "Young people need this time and sometimes even more to unwind, test out the environment, and adjust."

Two months later, school begins. Phoenix House is the only therapeutic community in this country with its own high school. A junior who drops out of his or her local high school is able to work and earn a regular high school diploma from Phoenix Academy at Shrub Oak. Again, the New York City Board of Education is a partner in this unique setting. Vocational education and training supplement the academic program. Those academically deficient and in their late teens may earn a General Education Diploma (GED), but they must go through the academic process like everyone else. This group especially needs social skills, patience, discipline, and the ability to follow a schedule. Like kids anywhere, all of them must learn to cope with the stresses of life.

There is flexibility in planning for a particular youngster, so not every individual is locked into the program outlined above. The Santa Ana community offers nine to twelve months of residential treatment, followed by a year of out-patient care. Education is a basic component of the program and family participation is required.

Another service provided by Phoenix House for young people is the Drug Prevention and Education service, which offers a three-session basic education program to public and private schools as well as seminars for faculty and parent groups. Although this unit operates primarily in the New York Metropolitan area, it has brought programs to schools through-out the country and has helped schools and communities in several states to design programs of their own.

FASTEP in Orange County, California, also provides drug education courses to public and private schools and operates an after-school family support program similar to the IMPACT program in New York.

HELPING ADULTS

Phoenix House has programs that are tailored to meet adults' needs. Among them is an out-patient evening program in New York City that provides therapy groups, counseling, and workshops to employed men and women whose use of drugs does not prevent them from functioning in society. Another called "Riverside" is a short-term cocaine residental program followed by out-patient services.

Long-term residential programs operate in six treatment centers, providing twenty-four-hour-a-day care, drug-free therapy, and a full range of rehabilitation services for some seven hundred residents. One important difference between the lives of teenagers and adults is that a great many functioning, working adults do not have a stable place to live. The staff finds that many stay with relatives, friends, or co-workers for varying lengths of time. A client without a permanent address adds to his or her history of instability and increases the difficulty in placing him or her in an appropriate program.

The retention rate at Phoenix House—that is, the proportion of clients who complete their treatment—is higher than at most comparable drug treatment programs, and a large percentage of those who complete treatment return to society and remain useful citizens.

In addition to restoring lives, the programs benefit the community by decreasing crime, keeping people out of prison, and turning out employable individuals who won't need welfare.

MANY CALL BUT FEW ARE TAKEN

Phoenix House has its limitations, and its programs are not designed to cure all of the ills of the world. The staff has to be exceptionally perceptive and selective in accepting and refusing applicants. In this way, Naomi's office serves as a gatekeeper. Senior and supervisory staff are often called upon to make difficult decisions, as is shown by the following two cases.

"But that's old stuff," said Annie. Annie was brought into Naomi's office by a counselor. The small-built, middle-aged woman had been interviewed a week earlier. In verifying her statements, it was discovered that Annie had not been entirely truthful. At the screening interview, Annie denied having a history of admissions to psychiatric hospitals. A follow-up review by staff revealed a different picture. When informed of these facts, Annie reluctantly admitted to maybe seven or eight admissions to mental hospitals . . . perhaps even more. She wasn't too sure. When reminded of the rule regarding full disclosure, Annie said, "But that's old stuff. It happened long ago. I'm interested in what can be done now." Naomi reminded Annie that all medical history is important to any plan for treatment. Annie still persisted with "I don't think it matters or makes any difference. The past is past." Although her last admission for attempted suicide had been less than a month ago, Annie didn't view it as important.

Naomi offered Annie several options, since her violations of the rule negated consideration for admission to Phoenix House. Annie readily agreed to return to Harlem Hospital Psychiatric Services, where she was known. Naomi made a telephone call to Harlem Hospital that would ease the admission process for Annie.

Three strikes and you're out, and that's what happened to Penny. She called for an appointment. Penny wanted to be readmitted. She was a former resident in the adult facility and left three times without permission. Over the telephone, Penny was petulant, charming, and appropriately repentant. She realized her mistake and promised to follow all Phoenix House rules in the future. Calmly, but firmly, Naomi repeated the rule that denies re-admission after such behavior. Pleas and tears did not move Naomi. Penny was referred to other treatment programs in Manhattan. Although Phoenix House cannot accept everybody who comes to them, they are able to send people to other treatment centers or hospitals. "When the staff is unable to help for whatever reason, appropriate referral is always made," says Naomi.

During 1985, the admission's staff saw face to face more then 4,500 people in day and night sessions. Usually there is a summer slump in admissions, but the 1986 crack epidemic prevented such a lull.

NETWORKING INTO THE COMMUNITY

Phoenix's admissions office serves the professional community in another vital way. It can provide data regarding trends and forecast changes in what's happening in the drug world. Naomi's staff knew a year ago that crack would cause a major catastrophe. "We knew of the violence involved with the drug, the degrading things women were doing to get drugs, and about the thievery. Parents could not give us telephone numbers, because their kids were stealing the telephones and selling them to get small packages of crack." A used telephone may bring one dollar or less on the street, guesses Naomi.

"Effective Parenting" is another much-needed service provided by the staff. This is offered as part of intervention sessions and by telephone. Naomi explains the need for such a service: "Parents have to stop being enablers. Without meaning to, they assist and encourage drug life-styles. They have to be told by counselors that it is all right to call the police or bar an out-of-control youth from the house. Parents who have never really disciplined their children or provided limits for unacceptable behavior cannot do an about-face when interacting with a six-foot, 190-pound teenager who is drugging. Parents feel guilty, physically threatened, and confused. Some know what has to be done but don't have the courage or strength to carry it out."

"Outreach" is yet another part of the admission staff's responsibility that is increasing in significance. The staff routinely visits hospitals' detoxification units to talk with patients and personnel in an effort to recruit clients for rehabilitation. Phoenix House also extends its interest and services to the criminal justice system and the courts and offers its programs as an alternative to imprisonment. Many first offenders and even repeaters are seventeen or eighteen years old and need medical help far more than prison sentences.

To extend outreach, especially to the young, radio and television "information spots" invite youngsters who are considering drugs or using drugs to call for an appointment to see a counselor.

Admissions is vital to the Phoenix House operation. But unfortunately, the admissions office only gets calls when there is a crisis and the caller has no where else to go. Much more needs to be done to educate the general public about the behavior of people who use drugs. "There are a lot of good people out there who are messing up their lives. They just don't realize the danger, and that's the hell of it," Naomi says with a deep sigh filled with resignation.

3

BREAKING

THE

CONNECTION

In this chapter, you will meet some young people who were able to "break the connection." Their stories are real, only their names have been changed to protect their identities.

In Chapter 2, you learned about a drug rehabilitation center called Phoenix House. But there are other facilities that accept young people for treatment. Daytop, Odyssey House, Teen Center, Steps to Recovery, Project Return, Damion, Reality House, Promesa, and Outreach House are among the better known in the Greater New York area.

OUTREACH HOUSE

The Reverend Coleman Costello, a Catholic priest, founded the project in 1980 to help reduce the rising number of young addicts in New York City. About 85 percent of the residents are from families where the parents or grandparents have problems with alcohol.

The project not only treats the youngster who has problems, but the whole family. Father Costello, who resembles a boxer in a round collar, says his congregation is in the schools, streets, and pocket parks of Queens. He finds them in all of the places kids gather to buy and use damaging chemicals to ease emotional pain. His crusades against drugs take place in both poor and upper middle-class communities. "The only difference is the latter have money, so drugs are easier to get."

Father Costello sees substance and alcohol abuse as the natural and inevitable consequence of a society that promotes the "easy out" and the "quick fix" as attractive solutions to personal difficulties. "Ironically," he says, "when young people first start using drugs, including alcohol, as a crutch, they are medicating themselves. But before they know it, the solution has turned into the problem. And they are more helpless than ever."

Daniel Lockspizer, a project counselor, reports that in the last four years, Outreach has counseled and referred for treatment about 25,000 young people from every corner of New York State. The project is one of the most successful treatment facilities for the very young—some are as young as twelve years. "Our success stories are attending colleges throughout the country. Other youngsters are gainfully employed in almost every vocation," says Lockspizer with pride.

Daytop

Daytop is dedicated to the idea of self-help. Daytop Village was the first program in the eastern United States to develop a method of treatment based on a drug-free residential community. The programs offered by Daytop can also be found in communities in Germany, England, Italy, Ireland, and the Philippines.

Daytop, like other facilities, places the addicted person in a tightly controlled environment. Honesty and openness are essential components in the process. Learning to identify and understand oneself and realize that drugs signal deeper inner conflicts are basic elements in Daytop's rehabilitative method. Staffed by a team of people with "street smarts" and committed ex-abusers and specialists, Daytop's approach is to convince

Fr. Costello at Outreach House with some of his successes in the class of '87.

users who believed real help was impossible that their lives can be changed for the better.

Daytop, formed in 1963, is the oldest and largest drug-free rehabilitation program in the United States. It has returned more than 40,000 individuals to the community as productive citizens.

PROMESA

Promesa is Spanish for "promise"—the promise of a future. This Hispanic, bilingual treatment community was founded 17 years ago to assist substance abusers in the New York City Metropolitan area in overcoming their physical and psychological dependence on drugs.

Treatment philosophy at Promesa draws upon the traditional values of the Puerto Rican family, characterized by a community-centered life based on the extended family, with support networks of relatives and friends.

Felix Velazquez, executive director, describes Promesa's objectives this way: "We take in addicts at a crisis point in their lives. With all addicts come a host of negatives: failed family and personal relationships; little or no structure in their life; feelings of inadequacy, of not belonging; and a generally fearful and pessimistic outlook.

"Our mission is to help them rebuild a life from the ground up—spiritually, morally, physically—through a comprehensive program designed to fit the particular needs that each person presents. Help is available from a team of highly trained professionals, therapists, medical clinicians, social workers, educators, and administrators. The plan includes health care, counseling, nutrition, legal assistance, and a decent place to live. It provides the traditional extended family network and a solid structure to support their rehabilitation. This tailor-made program is a contract between the clients and the Promesa family and consists of a series of logical steps designed to bring them along, at their pace, to a point where once again each person is whole, healthy, and able to perform a useful function in the greater society."

Like other programs, the individual is taught to accept responsibility for his or her actions, to shed a lifetime of dependency on others and to develop self-confidence. Later on, you'll read about CoCo, who changed her life at Promesa.

⬤DYSSEY HOUSE—MOTHERS PROGRAM

On Ward's Island, in New York City harbor, stands a building called MABON (Mothers And Babies Off Narcotics). The program operated from the multistoried tan building is called the Mothers Program. It is probably the only one of its kind in the United States.

MABON offers a residential treatment program for the pregnant addict and the addict parent with children under the age of five. There are always at least five pregnant women in the program. The mothers are between 18 and 36 years old, and some have up to three children.

"The program is not an easy one. It has a volunteer admissions policy that often attracts mothers who might have an ulterior motive—free child care. They are advised that parental involvement is a requirement. If they become AWOL [Absent Without Leave], the child is turned back to the authorities and the foster care system," says program director Veronica Thompson.

Residents share the responsibility for themselves, for the children, and for looking after their environment. It is also important for the parents to have constant discussions regarding feelings, slip-ups, and failure to keep agreements or live up to contracts. Open, mature communication is always encouraged.

The program is two-fold: Parents undergo treatment for their addiction and at the same time learn appropriate parenting skills. The Parents Program stresses growth and development in the parent-child relationship. Training is given by parent/child counselors and teachers, and there is individual, family, and marital counseling.

Kathy, discussed in this chapter, is a graduate of the Parents Program. Through its well-coordinated comprehensive education and training, she learned how to be a loving, capable, responsible parent and care for her two young sons.

The Parents Program helps families to re-enter society and to cease being dependent upon the therapeutic community. Some of those who have left the program have gone on to establish a family cooperative. These groups of single parents, their children, and nonparents live together and pool their resources for the benefit of all. They believe this arrangement provides a sense of security, companionship, and safety.

This re-creation of an extended family allows the adults most capable of outside employment to hold jobs, while the others care for the children and maintain the household. All live and work together. The co-op is self-sustaining. It does not rely upon the Parents Program for financial support, nor does it take help from welfare agencies.

The babies receive excellent care. Some of them are born addicted. Medical staff members monitor their development to detect physical and emotional problems as early as possible. Often children of drug abusers develop more slowly than other children of the same age. They may suffer from severe emotional and behavioral problems as young as six months. The Child Development staff designs a special program for each child to improve social, emotional, and cognitive abilities. Arts and crafts, science, drama, and play therapy are some of the many activities the program provides for the children. The Odyssey nursery, as it is known, stresses that children are a vital part of any community and that their well-being and proper development need to be the priority of the adults who live with them.

CAMELOT COUNSELING CENTERS

Camelot offers a combination of counseling and education services designed to meet the needs of drug-addicted teenagers. Many youngsters who become dependent on drugs have

A friendship between young people develops at Camelot.

had trouble "fitting in" with the rest of society. They may be missing school regularly or may be in trouble with the law. In addition to helping them control and eventually stop their drug use, Camelot provides counseling aimed at strengthening family ties and other relationships, and offers a variety of educational programs. Working together with the New York City Board of Education, the Centers have developed various types of vocational training that help clients begin a career as well as remedial education courses for those who have fallen behind in high school, or college equivalency programs.

Camelot centers are not residential, but operate on an "out-patient" basis. Counselors work to establish a personal relationship with their clients, based on mutual trust and respect. The centers also run family sessions, known as the Family Association of Camelot, which meet every week. Parents, guardians, or others closely involved with the client are required to attend.

TROUBLE IN PARADISE

Amy was born in a small New York State town twenty-one years ago. She was the fourth of five children. Family members enjoyed a happy relationship with each other and had no serious problems. Amy showed remarkable promise as a basketball player. Her older brothers coached her after school, and Amy became a member of the varsity high school team. Not only did she become a superb player, but she was an honor student as well.

Growing up in a small town offered Amy the warmth and friendliness of a small community, where the five thousand other residents were like an extended family. She remembers school closing when half of the 375 students had measles—although the mail carrier spoiled the holiday mood by delivering the lessons by hand. There was sleeping out-of-doors on hot starry nights, skinny dipping in the icy waters of Monshoe

Lake, and hooking spring salmon as they swam down from Canadian rivers. Winter skiing and summer hiking were part of the fun for the town's 134 adolescents. For Amy, it was drugs that spoiled this paradise.

NEIGHBORS' PARTIES

Drugs like alcohol and marijuana were introduced to Amy at neighbors' parties. Amy was fourteen and considered herself lucky to be invited to an older crowd's social events. This was the beginning of many parties, with many drugs and many blackouts. Looking back, Amy is amazed at the variety, the availability, and the low cost of drugs at that time. Parents felt safe . . . away from the muggers and street crime of the large cities. No one considered the possibility of drugs in this pastoral setting. Most adults drank alcohol, but this was expected in a small isolated town with a quiet social life, and no one considered alcohol a *real* drug.

THE PRESSURES OF A STAR

All through high school, Amy excelled in sports. She became a local legend with her high scoring at basketball tournaments. Alcohol and marijuana became increasingly important facets of her life. Although Amy's school work occasionally suffered and her grades slipped a little, no one, teachers or parents, seemed aware of the real state of affairs. In due time, Amy graduated with a 98-plus average and selected an athletic scholarship at a prestigious southern college. The pressures of college work, adjustment to a different cultural setting, and increased demands upon a star athlete escalated Amy's drug needs. There was no shortage of drugs at the college, and Amy was introduced to some new varieties. It was a great way to meet new friends and increase her popularity.

After her first year of college, Amy spent the summer vacation at home doing much of what she had done before . . . enjoying friends and drugs. But something was happening to her right knee—something quite serious. In her high school sophomore year, Amy had had an injury which was treated and assumed to have healed. Apparently, something had gone wrong. She needed more and more drugs just to get through a game. But Amy refused to seek medical help. If the knee was going, it meant the end of her reign as a star, and she found that idea unacceptable.

DRUGS ARE FREE

When school opened in September, Amy was still having problems with her knee. But kind and understanding doctors, coaches, and friends supplied her with pain killers and muscle relaxers. Playing basketball was the most important thing to her, and she couldn't conceive of life without it. After several months, stronger drugs replaced the muscle relaxers. Most of the drugs were free, because of her friendship with a doctor's son. Amy and the young man stole drugs and prescriptions from the doctor's busy clinic. The drugs were never missed. Amy and her friends became sellers and suppliers to others on campus.

THE BEGINNING OF THE END

Halfway through Amy's sophomore year, her father became seriously ill. She returned home to help with his care. Amy's mother, physically and emotionally involved with her husband's illness, wasn't aware of any change in her daughter's behavior. As a matter of fact, no one sensed any change in Amy. She still maintained that "homecoming queen" image.

Amy did not return to college. Instead she had major surgery on the knee during the summer. The doctors confirmed her greatest fear: Amy's career as a player was over. She was not convinced, and in September, Amy enrolled in another southern college to prove them wrong. But no matter how hard she tried, the knee would not work. Amy was devastated. It was the only positive identity she had—"the star, the best player."

Without it, she was nothing. Late one night, she packed her bags and, without notifying anyone, quickly and quietly left the campus.

AN EXTENDED HAND

Back home, it was easy for Amy to slip into her other identity—"getting high." Amy hung out with some new friends whom she met during the summer. They drank and used pot but never seemed to get high like Amy. Eventually Amy questioned them about her behavior. She wasn't happy with her life and wanted some direction. A drug education program in a nearby community college was suggested as a possible resource. Amy knew of the program and had attended it for a few weeks a couple of years earlier. The director offered her guidance, support, and encouragement. Amy enrolled in the program and met new drug-free young people who welcomed her into the group. These former abusers understood Amy's needs and could sustain Amy as she tried to make changes in her life.

DAYTOP—A THERAPEUTIC COMMUNITY

Part of the program's requirements was a two-week placement in a therapeutic community. Amy was sent to Daytop, probably the oldest such community in the United States. In retrospect, Amy feels that those two weeks were the most important of her whole life. While waiting for the admission interview, she considered her options. She could just walk through the two weeks, or she could use them to evaluate her own behavior and get herself back together. Amy chose the latter course.

GETTING HELP

Amy soon learned that her only chance of recovery was to seek aggressively for help. She spent every waking moment talking, questioning, and looking at and into her behavior. Amy became aware of how far she had strayed from that "small town girl makes good" image and why. The professional staff patiently worked with her and her new friends; they picked her up when she felt down. Amy was able to relive her desire to overdose while at college. She recalled taking a large quantity of drugs and lying on the bed sweating and trying to control her twitching limbs. She had made a conscious decision not to call for help, but to let the drug take over. Fortunately, Amy was rescued in time. The psychiatrist at Daytop helped her understand the despair and low self-esteem and self-image that can induce such suicidal behavior. Amy gained the strength needed to work through changes in many areas. She believes that her life actually began with those two weeks at Daytop. Completing a degree program at the community college made a significant difference, too.

Along the way, Amy decided to become a drug counselor. Daytop hired her at an entry level position. With her life under control, she was able to establish an identity for herself and determine what she wanted from her future. The staff, residents, and the program provided the environment, support, and encouragement to make this possible.

A MY'S ASSESSMENT

"It's easy to look back on your life and recognize the signals that had meaning . . . especially now that you know the signals," Amy says. Amy remembers that she always drank more than everyone else. Other kids would stop before the party was over, but Amy stopped only when there was nothing left to drink, smoke, or inject. Yet no one ever criticized her for overdoing it. Amy also recalls changes in her personality and behavior. There were incidents of irritability, short temper, lack of concentration, missed appointments, and failures of easy tests. But a star was permitted idiosyncracies.

No one criticized a champion, especially in a small town. It was easier to turn the other way or blame it on the pressures.

In high school, Amy frequently hung out in the hallways with other kids. Teachers and even the principal would chase the others back to class with threats of demerits or detention. But for Amy, there would be inquiries about her family's health and odds on the next game. Lateness to class and other minor violations were deliberately overlooked too. Even at home, family members were blind to everything except that all-American-girl image. Amy could do no wrong.

Perhaps intervention by family or school faculty would have at least called attention to what was happening and made her take a look at her behavior. Equal treatment would have toned down the stardom, too. But a lot of things permitted Amy's drugging to continue and escalate.

The adoration made it easy for Amy to avoid developing other significant parts of her life. Her family still has no knowledge of Amy's drug problem. If they even suspected there was one, they kept it well concealed. Amy's many trophies, medals, ribbons, citations, and plaques are lovingly displayed throughout the house.

INTERVENTION

Today, Amy is conducting intervention programs with high school kids. She is doing what could have helped her. Amy is helping youngsters identify areas in their lives that need attention. She spots the potential abuser, the kid with needs that aren't being met in school or at home and the kid who needs to bolster his or her self-image. Many of the fourteen- to eighteen-year-olds she works with are doing exactly what Amy did years ago. They are experimenting with everything, including the dangerous crack. Amy is helping them make positive and satisfying choices. She sees purpose in her life and enjoys every minute spent with her students. Having changed her own life, Amy hopes to make a difference to theirs.

Amy is aware of her own vulnerability. She is working toward a degree in social work, and to strengthen her motivation, she attends Alcoholics Anonymous. Close friends give her

*A*my and one of her young students watch a blue jay build a nest.

emotional support and encourage her efforts. There are still thoughts of getting high, but Amy knows how to handle these feelings now and is not threatened by them.

A MY'S RECOMMENDATIONS

Amy suggests that kids should build a strong sense of identity for themselves, and not base their lives on a single skill or talent. Amy was popular, revered, honored, and pampered all because of her athletic skill. Her only identity was that of a basketball star. When this was taken away, she perceived herself to be a nobody. Now she believes that feeling good about who you are and finding out about all the things you have to offer is the secret to happiness.

She is proud of herself and what she's accomplished. When she compares her values of several years ago to her present ones, she glows with delight. It used to be "playing ball." But, "My values now include honesty, truth, and friendships," she says. She has come a long way.

CLOTHES DO NOT MAKE THE MAN

It's hard to imagine that a healthy eleven-year-old American boy living in New York has never tasted a Big Mac, a pizza, the Colonel's breaded nuggets, or a Ball Park frank. But it's easier if you know Ali Shahid Abdul Wahhab. He is a Muslim. His parents raised 12 children in a large brownstone house in a middle-class section of Brooklyn. Ali has three older and three younger brothers, with five sisters scattered in between. Among family members, there is lots of love and affection. But there is also a strict adherence to the tenets of the Muslim religion.

BEING DIFFERENT HURTS

By the time Ali reached his third grade class, he was winded. He ran most of the way to avoid the bullies and teasers who seemed to lay in wait at every corner. Once inside the building, Ali hid in the coat room until the bell rang for classes.

Ali never complained about the beatings or indignities he suffered, which often made him wish that he was something else—perhaps a Catholic. He was tired of explaining why he didn't celebrate Christmas, Easter, Thanksgiving, or Mother's Day or salute the American flag. The kids laughed at his kufi, the round hat Muslims wear. At least once a week, Ali's khamis (a long coat) or dashiki (a colorful, pullover shirt) was ripped or soiled. Other kids spat on him, threw his kufi in the garbage can, or wrote abuse in chalk on his khamis. At lunch time, he remained in the classroom alone to eat a meal that his mother had carefully prepared for him. Ali was not permitted to eat lunch in the school cafeteria, because the menus often offered food forbidden to Muslims.

The isolation and indifference hurt the most. No one ever chose the "funny kid." If the teacher assigned him, his partner quickly and quietly drifted away to another group. Ali did not use swear words, even common ones. He was always too polite, too neat, and too clean to be real. He just didn't fit in with his noisy, active, urban classmates.

IT'S EASIER TO JOIN THEM

The religious doctrines of love, nonviolence, trust, and fidelity had been woven into Ali's personality since birth. But it was becoming harder and harder to accept this treatment. Ali was large for his age, so it was natural for him to consider using his size and strength to get attention and respect. Ali became a bully. It worked so well that he began to act like some of his peers. Once he removed his kufi and dashiki and used their street language, he felt comfortable. He was no longer an outsider. For the first time, he had friends. He was accepted!

Ali left his quiet neighborhood to hang out with his new friends and their role models. These young adults were number bankers, mules or messengers, hustlers, drug dealers, pimps, or gang leaders. They had power and money. Street fighting, petty thievery, and sneaking into local theaters where films featuring violence, mayhem, and brutality were shown became a weekly habit. Many of these were low-budget "Grade C" movies featuring stereotyped images of macho minority men, which impressed youngsters. Ali admired these heavy types and tried to imitate them.

POT AND THE NINTH GRADE

Ali smoked his first weed, or "gonza" as the kids called it, in the first year of junior high school. He was eleven years old. Ali was amazed to find classmates who smoked four to five nickel bags everyday. They smoked alone or with other kids. By his twelfth birthday, Ali couldn't sleep unless he had smoked five bags and couldn't eat without inhaling a joint first. Ali now believes marijuana is a more serious problem for kids than adults realize.

Before he was into his teens, Ali began to move up the criminal ladder. He replaced his old role models with new ones—felons, murderers, arsonists, and burglars. He listened intently to their daring exploits, no matter how exaggerated they were. Ali admired their courage and risk-taking. Talking with them was more exciting than any movie.

Ali went to school sporadically, but he only attended Physical Education classes. In the middle of the tenth grade, he left school. Ali spent most days playing hooky at parties held in the apartments of kids whose parents were at work. At these partics, truants smokcd marijuana and drank bccr all day long.

MORE DRUGS, MORE CRIME

Ali's need for money and drugs and the desire to emulate his new heroes resulted in a neighborhood crime wave. Ali carefully selected working couples' homes and broke into them during the morning hours. In the afternoon, he hung around the school yard. Once, a security guard noticed Ali loitering and called the police, who searched him. They found $250 in his jeans, along with ten dollars worth of marijuana. The police thought they had a drug peddler, but in fact Ali had got the money by selling a copy machine stolen from a real estate office near his home.

Near the end of the school year, Ali ran away for two weeks. He lived in a drug factory where he and another teenager sold marijuana. He spent his money on fancy clothes and jewelry. He wanted to create the image of a "big shot." The third week, the loft was raided and Ali was arrested. His bewildered but loving parents bailed him out and brought him home. It was a shocking experience for Ali. During the raid, he was caught in a cross fire. Bullets whizzed by Ali's right ear as he flattened himself against a wall.

EXTENDED VACATION

Ali spent his next two years as a typical high school dropout. He played handball and basketball most of the day. Money for beer and marijuana was provided by committing acts of shoplifting, petty thievery, and "boosting" (selling stolen items). At times, Ali earned money legitimately by unloading trucks. There was less tension in this, because the police would not hassle him as a potential criminal suspect. But never the less, the money always went for his daily pot, new flashy clothes, and more jewelry. Ali's companions were, like himself, dropouts from school—and life.

Once, Ali did enroll in a General Education diploma course. It was the alternative to being thrown out of home. Ali's mother was losing patience and was discouraged with Ali's lack of motivation in either learning or working. But Ali didn't complete the course.

ANOTHER CHANCE, ANOTHER DRUG

After a family conference, Ali's father suggested a possible apprenticeship in the construction industry. It had provided an excellent living for him and his family. He could also ease the entrance process for Ali's union membership. Ali began as a demolition laborer. Within two months, his salary rose to $1,500 a week. And he was only 17 years old.

With his pockets stuffed with fifty-dollar bills, Ali swaggered through his new neighborhood. He considered himself "top choice"—nobody could touch him. All he needed now was a car and better jewelry. He didn't have to steal anymore either. Ali's life revolved around drugs and stylish and expensive clothes. This new life-style also called for a new drug.

Some of his new associates were involved in serious crime, including murder. An increasing number of his former classmates were either in prison or in the cemetery. This frightened Ali enough to destroy his fascination with criminal types. But his drugging continued.

At a birthday party, a pretty teenager dared Ali to sniff cocaine, and he accepted. He wanted to impress the young girl with his bravado. Ali used marijuana daily during the week. But on the weekend, cocaine soon became the "thing to do." The cocaine high was intense, but crashing left Ali drained. He tried everything and anything to reduce his need for the drug, but nothing worked. Nevertheless, Ali continued to look fit and strong. Now he laughs about the irony of this situation. As a Muslim, his diet was mostly of fresh vegetables and fruits, fish, and whole wheat products. He did not drink whiskey, nor did he regularly drink beer. Ali believes his diet helped to maintain adequate nutrition for the strenuous demands of the construction job and the destructive effects of the drugs.

Ali's major concern was his need to increase the amount of cocaine necessary to reach a euphoric high. Within three months, Ali went from a twenty-dollar-a-day to a three-hundred-dollar-a-day habit. Often, a week's salary was spent two days after payday. With no other income, Ali was forced to sell his clothes for drug money. At first, it was the fancy silk shirts, British Jax slacks and camel-hair jackets. His prized leather suits and sheepskin coats were sold next.

Ali was depressed and disgusted about his lack of control. After work, he returned home and sat in his darkened room crying. He envisioned his life slipping away. He likened it to watching escaping sand in an hourglass. But he could not invert the hourglass and start anew.

ENTER CRACK

A friend invited Ali to a marathon party (one which may last two or three days depending upon the amount of drugs available). Ali smoked crack for the first time and was thrilled with the sensation. Within a short time, Ali had a treble addiction. Between crack, cocaine, and marijuana, he was spending huge amounts on drugs. Ali withdrew money from his savings to pay drug bills that were now more than four hundred dollars a day.

Although most of Ali's expensive wardrobe was gone, he still managed to keep two cherished sheepskin suits. One day, he was freebasing with some neighborhood guys and needed more crack. Ali went home and got his suits. One of his brothers saw him leaving the house and decided to follow Ali. He observed Ali from a short distance, and saw him selling the suits for $20 each. Ali's brother knew the suits cost $1200 each when new. When Ali's brother objected to the sale, a fight followed. Ali ran home before the police arrived. He did not want his brother to become involved with addicts and their world.

As he lay on his bed, Ali felt disgusted and humiliated. He had shamed his family name and reputation. He remembered that he had hidden his sister's bicycle behind the closet door, planning to sell it later. With a sickening feeling of disgust, he returned the bicycle to the basement. He threw himself on his bed and sobbed uncontrollably. He was no longer in charge of his actions. His behavior was controlled by drugs. Ali cried out for help.

After an hour of emotional and physical release, Ali telephoned Phoenix House for an appointment. He didn't discuss his plans with anyone. But he told his father, "I'm going into a program. I need help. I cannot handle large sums of money, so I'm quitting my job." His father didn't ask any questions, but Ali sensed the older man's support. When his father visited him a month later in the Shrub Oak residential facility, he held Ali close to him. Ali was assured that he was on the right course at last.

ALI'S ASSESSMENT

"Without my religious upbringing, I would not be alive today," Ali says. He used to think that his problems began with his strange clothes and a religious upbringing that was too strict. But now he says, "I had to learn to love myself and my religion . . . to be comfortable with who and what I am. Instead, I tried to be what was popular, attractive, and faddish. I didn't believe in myself and lacked the strength of my convictions.

"My parents would have helped, but I didn't trust anyone. But they apparently never doubted me. They were like a security blanket. They didn't say much, but they were always there."

Ali earned an academic diploma during his two years' residency at Phoenix House. He is interested in attending college, and has investigated a career in psychology or counseling. He thinks that he would be of help to other young people. The warmth, professionalism, and friendliness of the counselors at Phoenix House was significant in helping Ali help himself.

The structure of the program and his religion both helped bring order into Ali's life. Daily reading in the Koran reinforced his earlier family training in religious doctrines. He thinks that religious principles can help everyone, especially kids.

These principles are from the Koran, but can help anyone:

1. God is first above everything.
2. Life as we live it here on earth is materialistic and temporary.

Ali on the job thinks of the future with optimism.

3. God rewards every act that is positive.
4. Avoid negative feelings.
5. All people have options. They can choose to do right or wrong.

Ali doesn't try to be anyone but himself these days. He continues follow-up counseling sessions at Phoenix House. He is enrolled in drama class at the Double Image Theater in Manhattan, a troupe associated with John Jay College. Working and acting there have improved his diction, communication skills, and poise. He is also able to express in drama things that often cannot be articulated clearly. Ali has found the true meaning of friendship and can enjoy a drug-free party. Ali says, "The only way to prove something to yourself is from the inside out and not from the outside in."

His parents are very happy to regain their son. Ali's mother smiles and says, "Well, one out of twelve ain't bad."

CURTAIN GOING UP?

The mass of honey-colored hair appears to be three feet long in any direction. When she throws the wild mane back from her pretty face, the rooster comb of spiky hair resembles the crown made famous by Miss Liberty. But this is no statue! The crowd is applauding CoCo's dance performance to the highly charged jazz piano tunes of Willie ("the Lion") Smith.

CoCo's style is inspirational, with an infusion of tap, ballet, African, and modern. The flashes of silver and red in her highly styled outfit merge with her natural animal energy and furious toe work. With one final series of swiveling gyrations, this dazzling star's performance ends and without waiting for the house lights to go up, the crowd stands. The applause is deafening—growing louder and louder. CoCo bows low and weeps with happiness. The noise is thundering and coming closer. It awakens her. For a brief moment, CoCo is confused.

And then she realizes that the sounds are the familiar sirens of police cars heard regularly in El Barrio. CoCo has been having her favorite recurrent dream. She lies on the cot trembling and perspiring. The dream always leaves her exhausted.

CoCo is a former crack abuser. She is completing a year's treatment and residency at Promesa, a therapeutic community in the Bronx, a borough of New York City where she grew up. CoCo is a nickname given to this attractive and exotic looking seventeen-year-old by her West Indian–born grandmother. As an infant, CoCo's first gurgling sounds reminded the old woman of the cooing sugar birds in Barbuda, a small island in the Caribbean. The birds eat sugar left on outdoor dining tables.

CoCo's recurrent dream helps keep alive some hope for a future. There were so many "fox traps" in CoCo's path, according to her grandmother. To begin with, the youngster never knew her real father because he abandoned the family before her birth. CoCo's mother and stepfather drank heavily and abused her physically and psychologically for years. CoCo's mother, handicapped by cerebral palsy, has a nervous disorder. CoCo believes that she wasted much of her life trying to find happiness in socially unacceptable ways. But she blames no one.

Most of CoCo's early care was provided by her maternal grandmother. By the age of six, CoCo was strong-willed, assertive, and difficult to handle. She could be charmingly manipulative and was highly intelligent. Within the next four years, CoCo was able to assume much of the responsibility for caring for herself.

A RUNAWAY AT FOURTEEN

This attitude of independence led to many arguments between mother and daughter. The more self-sufficiency CoCo demonstrated, the closer her mother attempted to draw the reins. CoCo refused to honor curfews, do chores, or listen to her parents' advice about anything. As both parents increased their drinking, their marital relationship deteriorated. CoCo found the hostile and abusive environment unbearable and left home at the age of fourteen. She did not return again until after her seventeenth birthday, and that was only for a two-week stay.

Like many runaways, CoCo never lived more than twenty blocks away from her home during those years. She saw her parents occasionally, but they were not happy meetings. Accusations, name-calling, and physical abuse were features of these volatile confrontations. CoCo stayed with friends (boys, girls, or both), homeless people in abandoned buildings or shelters, in welfare hotels, subways, and doorways. To support herself, CoCo worked as cashier, salesperson, and counter girl. Her clothes were borrowed, stolen, and shared with other kids who were also runaways, drifters, emancipated minors, or homeless. No matter what or where her bed might be, CoCo snuggled against a soiled, faded, tattered stuffed lion with most of his shaggy mane missing. Lenny, as CoCo called him, was her prized possession . . . a gift from the only person she ever trusted—a now dead grandmother.

*S*CHOOL—ONE SAFE PLACE

Although she was without a home, life at school didn't change very much. CoCo felt comfortable and accepted there. She also felt safe for a few hours. CoCo was absent more than the previous year, but her average never fell below 80 percent. She loved the challenge of classwork and the stimulation of competition. English was her favorite subject, especially literature. Often late at night, CoCo would find a quiet corner and read a paperback like *Crisis Down Under,* a historical novel of South Africa's apartheid. CoCo's teachers encouraged her questions and contributions to classroom discussions. She always wanted to know more. Ideas expressed in her poetry and short stories, especially those about foreign cultures, revealed a sincere quest for knowledge and understanding. When called the "thinker" by other kids, CoCo would try to defend her sincere curiosity.

But this only increased the differences between "her" and "them." "You think too much," they teased. But CoCo's thoughts were on a possible future as a dancer, journalist, or anthropologist. Sometimes, she thought she might be good at all three.

FROM CIGARETTES TO COCAINE

CoCo's parents have a mostly "off and on" type of marriage, she reveals. In between, there are her mother's boyfriends—sometimes living in and sometimes not. It was one of these friends who gave CoCo her first cigarette and drink of beer when she was eleven years old. He was eighteen.

After several years of cigarettes, CoCo progressed to smoking pot. Then, a few weeks before her sixteenth birthday, CoCo used cocaine for the first time. Her new boyfriend, Jimmie, paid twenty-five dollars for a small package of white powder. After inhaling the drug, they went to a popular disco and CoCo danced for hours. She loved the freedom the drug seemed to give her. Every weekend, CoCo and Jimmie sniffed coke and then went dancing. CoCo was a star. Other dancers stopped and circled them while the flashy pair executed tricky routines. CoCo loved the attention, the excitement, and the adoration.

Suddenly it was spring and more people were on the street. Everyone was talking about a new high that was the ultimate. The drug was called crack, a form of cocaine. CoCo was anxious to try it. Jimmie shared his pipe with her. Like others, CoCo became addicted quickly. Since she had no money, she went home and stole from her mother's purse. CoCo also took food stamps, jewelry, clothes, and radios. Her personality changed and she became abusive and antagonistic to anyone who tried to help her. The mother-daughter relationship worsened, as their verbal disagreements escalated to shouting matches. Her mother changed the locks so CoCo couldn't get into the apartment.

CRACK TAKES OVER

By the end of her junior year, CoCo had flunked out of school because of her repeated absences. She wasn't able to take her SATs, and plans for college were forgotten. Meanwhile, she lost twenty pounds and her clothes hung like draperies around a reed-thin body. Her once flawless, almond-colored skin was sallow and lifeless. Deepening dark circles ringed vacant staring eyes that used to sparkle and glisten with excitement and expectation. But beyond her physical condition, CoCo didn't like what was happening to her sense of values. Too often, she found herself in places and with people whom she formerly considered "scum." They were pickpockets, drug dealers, prostitutes, and street people. Some were violent and others were mentally or emotionally disturbed. To pay for her drugs, CoCo worked in seedy massage parlors, pornographic cinemas, and for third-rate escort service agencies. For a while, she sold "sex over the telephone" to anonymous callers. At times, she stayed in *bonzo* houses, or crack factories, because there was no other place to go.

The addiction controlled her life. In order to buy crack, CoCo often went to high-crime neighborhoods where the drug was available on tenement rooftops. The location could change several times a night. One night, CoCo climbed the stairs alone to six different rooftops before she found action. CoCo was so desperate that she took more crack than usual. She was found unconscious, propped up against a garbage can on a Bronx street by a police officer. At Lincoln Hospital, CoCo received emergency treatment and was admitted for additional medical care after she regained consciousness.

All of the next day, CoCo lay quietly in the narrow hospital bed reviewing the last six months of her life. Everything was wrong. Her mother was acutely ill in the hospital. Jimmie was in prison serving an eighteen-month sentence. She had flunked out of school. She had no place to go. She had no real friends. Two days later, CoCo was discharged from the hospital. A social worker gave her five dollars and directions to Promesa. CoCo didn't hesitate. It was the only place to go.

THE WAR IS OVER

"Professionals would say that I belong to a 'high risk group,' " CoCo says. An alcoholic parent, unstable family structure, and an unsatisfactory mother-daughter relationship were CoCo's risk factors. The need to belong to someone, to get attention and be recognized, to be better than others, and the inability to postpone gratification were also influential in her drugging.

CoCo's mother visited her twice in six months. The first visit was reluctant, distant, and cool. But they managed to talk more openly the second time. Because CoCo had experienced pain herself, she now had a deeper understanding of what her mother had lived with and why she had chosen the ways she did to cope with despair and hopelessness.

Although her mother still resents CoCo's independence, she appears to be proud that CoCo has taken charge of her life. They negotiated a truce. CoCo will not hassle her mother about drinking alcohol. In turn, her mother will respect CoCo's plan to go to an out-of-town college and live independently of her.

There were no tears, no hugs, and no touching. But a look of mutual admiration exchanged between them signified that the war was over. They were both growing up at last.

One year of therapy at Promesa helped CoCo learn a great deal about herself. "A lot of it I didn't like . . . like being insecure and feeling inadequate. That's why I liked to be a snob, put people down, and show off." There are other signs of progress. CoCo regained her lost weight and physically is in good health again. She is beginning to like the new CoCo and is returning to high school to prepare for college entrance within a year.

Most of CoCo's relationships with peers and others were superficial. She understands that she avoided real and close involvements with classmates, because of her fear of being rejected. "I could put others down, but I wanted to be loved by everyone. I could take, but I couldn't give. I think I'm ready to open up to friendships now."

CoCo still has other fears to conquer. Will she be strong

enough to prove herself in a strange, distant college environment? How will she deal with loneliness and frustration? What kind of man will fit into her new life-style? These are only a few of the challenges ahead for this beautiful teenager. Intensive counseling and guidance will continue to help her find her way. At college, she will live with a family, instead of in the dormitory, for additional emotional support and protection. Her academic course load will be limited for a while. CoCo will have a part-time job too, so she can earn some money for herself.

But as CoCo looks around the walls of her room, decorated with photographs of rock stars with stylish clothes, dancers, models with the latest makeup and hair styles, she realizes that it is only she who can determine if and when that "curtain" will be going up.

DOES ANYONE WANT ME?

Even as the war against drugs continues to accelerate, the number of new addicts keeps growing. Unfortunately, many of them are younger than eighteen. Robin is an example of a new and growing subpopulation among the addicted. At 16, the child of drug-using parents *and* grandparents, she is both a second and third generation addict. "It goes like this," the director of her treatment agency said. "Robin is of Hispanic origin. When she was a baby, her father left their home. Within a few years, Robin's mother married a Jewish man. After a year of marriage, Robin's mother chose to separate herself from her husband and Robin. Subsequently, Robin's stepfather married a Jewish woman who insisted Robin be adopted by them. Her biological parents, her adoptive parents, and their parents all have been treated for chemical abuse."

LONELY IN A CROWD

With so many marriages and divorces, children like Robin have half sisters and stepbrothers. Robin has both, but there are no blood-related kin in her current household. Her favorite was a stepbrother, who was seventeen. They shared secrets occasionally, especially when Robin's behavior caused family arguments and no one was speaking to Robin.

Both of Robin's stepparents work. Her stepmother is a registered nurse and her stepfather is a court officer. The family of six enjoy a comfortable, middle-class life-style. But Robin never felt comfortable at home. She is lonely. "They have each other. I am the odd one," she complains. Robin's parents tried to make her happy with expensive clothes, jewelry, and special treatment, but her sense of isolation only increased. Heated arguments became a daily occurrence. At night, Robin held Charley tightly to her chest and cried herself to sleep. Charley, an old loppy-eared, gray stuffed elephant, was the only stable thing in her life. He had been with her since she was a baby. At age thirteen, Robin was a freshman in high school. She had an enviable academic record. But Robin found school and teachers boring.

A TYPICAL DAY

Robin caught the bus on the corner at 8:00 each school day, then changed to another bus at Tremont Plaza, and arrived at Madison High School at 8:40. She went to English 6, and then reported to her homeroom for attendance check. Then Robin walked out a side door. By 10:30, she was in the back room of a candy store with other kids who should have been in school too. Alcoholic beverages were free, if you bought pot, cocaine, or mescaline. The kids spent most of the day hanging out there . . . drinking, smoking, and snorting.

Robin saw her biological mother about once every four months. They usually met unexpectedly on the street. Over a sandwich in a nearby delicatessen, they argued about her school work, truancy, and shabby appearance. Her mother, unaware of Robin's drug habit, gave her money for clothes and visits to the beauty parlor. Robin didn't care about her appearance. She used the money to buy cocaine and pot.

At home, Robin stole from the younger children's banks and took grocery money hidden in the kitchen cabinet. When her stepparents sent her out to buy an item, Robin would get a much cheaper brand or version and pocket the difference. Soon Robin stopped pretending that she was enrolled in school. She lounged around the house all day and drank to get drunk. When she was drunk, Robin didn't feel the pain of rejection and loneliness. She didn't shower, shampoo her hair, or change her clothes. At night, Robin went to some of the seedier parts of the city where young prostitutes could earn up to six hundred dollars a night. Just before dawn, Robin would taxi home with hundreds of dollars stuck down in her tiny shorts. She felt dirty. Robin explains, "I felt like a dog in heat. Sometimes when I came home, I would shower for 30 minutes trying to get rid of that feeling, but it would still be there to bother me, until it was time to go back to the streets."

ATTEMPTS TO INTERVENE

Robin's mother received a letter from a dean at Madison High. It was the first official notice of her daughter's status at the school since Robin became a truant. The low grades and absences shocked her. A nasty confrontation followed with crying and screaming by both. Robin's mother made an appointment for Robin to see a psychiatrist. She kept only three appointments. "He was okay, but he didn't understand me. Really, I think that he was more interested in my queer family setup than in me."

Robin's maternal grandmother tried to help her too. At 62, she still used cocaine occasionally. She told Robin about a treatment agency that had helped her. But Robin wasn't interested.

When medical intervention failed, an aunt suggested that Robin stay with her. Aunt Sylvia was 38 years old and knew all about drugs, since she was a former heroin and cocaine abuser. Aunt Sylvia had been a hippie twenty years earlier. She gave Robin money for drugs to keep her from prostituting herself. Meanwhile, she tried to talk Robin into reducing the amount of alcohol she consumed each day. Robin and her aunt went shopping for expensive and attractive clothes and shoes. They went to movies and the theater and ate in fancy restaurants. Despite all of this, Aunt Sylvia could not break through the wall of distrust Robin felt toward all adults. After three months, Robin went back to the streets.

Robin's stepparents walked the streets of the neighborhood trying to find their daughter. They talked to bartenders, delicatessen and liquor store clerks. The photo of the fresh-faced girl that they held up for them to see bore little resemblance to the thin, pale, dirty kid they knew. But they didn't give up. They followed up every lead. They blamed themselves. Robin had too many adjustments to make, because the adults in her life kept changing partners. She didn't resemble them either. Her olive skin and curly, dark hair contrasted sharply with the rest of the family's fair skin and straight, titian-colored hair. Both parents had histories of drug use. They were former "flower children" themselves. They knew Robin couldn't kick her habit without help. So they continued their nightly search. At times, their paths almost crossed.

THE LAST TIME

They didn't find Robin. She found them. One afternoon, Robin needed money for crack. She came home to steal some money. Robin had lost more than 20 pounds and was malnourished and tired. She remembered that money was often kept in a box in her parents' bedroom closet. Robin tried to lift several heavy suitcases to reach the box. In her weakened condition, she couldn't move them. Robin grew dizzy and faint, before collapsing on the floor. Two hours later, her stepmother found her lying there. The ambulance took Robin to the emergency room at St. Elizabeth Hospital. She was admitted to the Detoxification Unit for treatment.

GRADUATION

Robin graduated from high school in June 1986. She is attending a small liberal arts college in the western part of the country and doing well. She is no longer lonely and has many friends among her peers and adults at the college. Robin has finally progressed to a better life. The recovery process is not easy. She attends Alcoholics Anonymous (AA) meetings three times a week. Robin also sees a psychiatrist monthly. Only Robin's counselor is aware of her past. "Since I don't have drugs to blame, I have to take the responsibility for my own behavior. I am experiencing feelings that I never knew before, like love, caring, and sharing. I'm living proof that people can change," she says. Robin lives in a dormitory with other young women and some male students. She tells of the pot smoking and cocaine snorting in which some of them engage. "Funny, it doesn't bother me. I like myself now and nothing could change that."

Robin's friends are drug-free too. She has learned to trust them, as well as adults. Her stepparents have been supportive. They are attending AA and Narcotics Anonymous meetings. Their long-distance telephone calls are frequent and lengthy, and full of love and concern for her. They speak of plans for vacations and encourage Robin to maintain her A average. When she has a problem or a bad day, Robin feels comfortable calling them. "We talk it out and find a satisfactory solution." For a brief moment, a serious look erases her wide smile. "Just think, I once wanted to kill myself, because my life was empty and everything was so ugly. I would have missed all of this," she concludes in a plaintive tone.

Robin has this advice to give to other teenagers: "Tell someone about your problem. Keeping things bottled up inside of you only makes you look for something to ease the pain, and drugs will do it. Tell a friend, teacher, or guidance counselor if you don't feel comfortable talking with your parents. But tell somebody, please!"

TAKE MY HANDS

"With the words, 'Take my hands,' I rejoined the human race," says Genna Maitland. "I reached out to my three kids—Keva, 15, Anna, 13, and Danny, 10, as we knelt at the foot of my bed. Each of us clutched a string of rosary beads." In a raspy, tear-choked voice, Genna stumbled through her version of the Lord's Prayer. The kids stared in disbelief. Was this another game, a joke? They couldn't believe this pothead who cared more about getting high than anything else. What was she up to now?

HISTORY REPEATS ITSELF

The kids were right. She had not been a good mother. It may have been that way because Genna didn't have a good mother either. Her parents were alcoholic; and up to the age of 8, she didn't even know them. Genna was raised by her grandparents, whom she considered her parents. When her grandmother became ill, Genna was sent to live with her real parents. It was difficult to adjust to these strangers' life-styles, which consisted of arguing, fighting, and drinking. Genna resisted calling them "Mom" and "Dad." She also resented the many hours spent alone while they enjoyed themselves in a neighborhood bar. There were other times when she was unexpectedly left with her parents' friends, relatives, or neighbors for indefinite periods.

At 14, Genna became curious about that liquid that could make a person happy, sad, or combative. She decided to taste some gin. Surprisingly, Genna liked the taste. But more importantly, the resulting mood change was delightful. Genna adopted the drinking patterns of her parents, and by age 17, she was ready to join them on their nightly ventures to the bar.

NEW PRESSURES, NEW DRUGS

One night, Genna met a tall, charming, and handsome drinking partner. Within a month, they were married—on Genna's eighteenth birthday. Both kids thought that it would be a fun thing to do, since they were attracted to each other. Love and commitment were never mentioned by either of them. But Genna, happy in her new role, thought she would never be lonely again. Although Genna worked as a teacher and part time as a beautician, she and her new husband spent several nights a week with the regulars at the bar. They continued to drink heavily, often as much as a fifth of vodka a day.

Within five years, the Maitlands had three children. Genna had mixed feelings about being a mother. She was proud of her self-imposed discipline; while pregnant, she never took any drugs. But child care and housework brought new responsibilities that Genna was not prepared to handle. Charlie became abusive when meals were late, laundry not done, and when the apartment was untidy and dirty. He often struck Genna or the children. To ease her feeling of inadequacy, fear, and despair, Genna turned to cocaine and pot.

The children were frequently left to manage on their own. Groceries were charged at a local store or borrowed from neighbors. Meanwhile, Genna's drug bills were rising and her unemployment added pressure to the family's need for more money. So Charlie turned to crime.

COCAINE AND CAREFREE

An inebriated thief usually bungles the job, and that was Charlie's fate. He was sent to prison for a minimum of six years. Without Charlie's nagging, punches, and slaps, Genna felt free. She spent even more time at the bar getting drunk and using any drug that was available. One morning she awoke in the seedy, rundown hotel room of a stranger. They had met the preceding night in a club that was known for the high quality of its pot. He invited Genna to accompany him to Jamaica, West Indies. She readily accepted. A trip to celebrate her new freedom was just what she needed, Genna rationalized. She had a bank balance of about three thousand dollars and a close girlfriend. Together these would take care of the children's needs. After a quick call to her friend, Genna and her new playmate were taxiing to Kennedy airport.

Lazy days spent on the endless sun-swept beaches gazing at tranquil blue-green waters were perfect for sampling home-grown pot and Bolivian cocaine. After a week of fun and surf, Genna's companion deserted her. She had no money, so she sold the few pieces of jewelry that she owned. One of the hotel maids offered Genna a room in an already overcrowded cottage. Genna accepted gratefully. Luckily she had a return airplane ticket to the states. But since Genna had little else, she earned money by prostitution and selling drugs to tourists. She received drugs, at a low cost, for her personal use.

THE PARTY'S OVER

Sometimes Genna spent the nights lying on the beach gazing up at the dark sky. It was almost a month since she'd seen or thought about her children. But sometimes at night Genna would have nightmares and see the kids at the foot of her small bed. In her cocaine stupor, she'd hear them crying, "Momma where are you? Momma come home!" When these dreams began to occur too frequently, Genna decided to sleep on the beach.

One night, after a day filled with disappointment, rejection, and loneliness, Genna lay on the beach. As she stared through tear-filled eyes, she thought of a line by Ralph Waldo Emerson. "When it is dark enough, you can see the stars." Genna repeated this several times to herself. She was thinking clearly for the first time in months. Not only could she see the stars but she could see her future. And it was as dark as the navy blue sky above.

Occasional meals of junk food, limited hours of sleep, and

chemical abuse made Genna lose weight and her good looks as well. She was a beach bum with an unattractive sallow tan and freckles. Genna's blonde, sun-bleached hair needed cutting and styling. She didn't recognize the masklike face in the mirror anymore. Genna was tired. "The party is over and it is time to go home," she mumbled. Her Jamaican friends rescued her again by calling an aunt and uncle in Miami. They were happy to learn that Genna was alive. Her children had been sent down to them when the three thousand dollars had been spent and Genna's friend tired of babysitting.

TAKING STOCK

At the airport, Genna's looks shocked her aunt and uncle. They decided to make some improvements before Genna met her children, who were staying with them. A stop at the beauty parlor and a boutique helped a great deal. Although thin, Genna did look presentable. The children were ecstatic and wanted to know where she had been. The adults decided it was best to say that Genna had been hospitalized for an infection. But Keva was suspicious and avoided making eye contact with her mother. She wasn't fooled by Genna's lie. She had heard so many of them.

KEVA STRIKES BACK

Keva's anger and hostility toward her mother grew stronger. She asked herself, "Why do I have such no-good parents? What have I done to deserve them?" Once the family was back in New York, Genna went to work part-time and Keva cared for the children while Genna bar-hopped evenings. During Christmas week, there was a special family day at the prison and Genna took Keva to see her father. Even in jail, her parents argued. Keva was disgusted, embarrassed, and angry.

The next day, Keva drank a fifth of vodka. Only nine years old, she became very sick. At the hospital, the doctor told Genna that only the vomiting had saved Keva's life. Afterward, when sober, Keva remembered the good feeling she got from the vodka, so it became her favorite drink. Within a year Keva was using pot too. The failing grades, poor attendance, and unruly behavior resulted in the loss of Keva's scholarship in a private school.

DRUGS HERE, THERE, AND EVERYWHERE

Keva enrolled in a public school. She had no problem finding other kids who drank and smoked pot. Keva and her new friends would meet in a park near the school and fill empty apple juice or orange juice cartons with whiskey. During class, they sipped the whiskey through straws. By the age of 12, Keva had escalated her drug use to include PCP (angel dust) and mescaline. Keva sat through classes in a half-conscious state, often falling off her chair to the floor. The kids laughed, but not the teacher. Security guards weighing as much as 250 pounds attempted to carry Keva to the principal's office. Keva fought back with almost equal strength. When the principal asked her about drug use, Keva kicked him in the groin. Ironically, they shared the same ambulance to the hospital. The principal was treated in the emergency room and Keva was sent to the Detoxification Unit.

After five days, Keva was released from the hospital. But the school would not re-admit her to classes. So she found other dropouts and went back to using pot and alcohol. Keva's drinking now matched her mother's, whose drinking and cocaine use led to the loss of employment and help from social services.

NOW I LAY ME DOWN TO WEEP

Genna watched Keva become a younger version of herself. Genna hated herself for what she was doing to her child. At 14,

Keva was addicted to pot and alcohol and soon would turn to prostitution. Did she want this for Keva? Each night, Genna's pillow was wet with tears as she prayed for strength to turn the family around. Her mother was dead now, and her husband in prison. She turned to her relatives in Florida for help. They convinced Genna that she didn't need to punish herself any longer. So there was no need for drugs to suppress the pain. She had a right to use her talents and be a useful member of society. With their encouragement and support, Genna entered a treatment program and spent seven months in a halfway house.

The younger children went to Florida to live with relatives. Keva remained in New York, but attended Camelot Counseling Services for three months before joining her siblings in Florida. In a new and stable environment, Keva stopped using drugs. She went to school part-time at first, but within three months, Keva could manage a full day.

When Genna was released, the children came back home. Genna's counselor recommended therapy for everyone, especially Keva. In addition to Alcoholics Anonymous for Genna and Keva, and Alateen, a program for the children of alcoholics, for Anna and Danny, psychiatric family counseling was planned for everyone. The sessions are held three times a week and will continue for as long as necessary.

TAKE MY HANDS

Genna's sobriety gave her strength and the desire to make a new life for herself and the kids. But she needed help . . . the children's help, especially Keva's. "If they support each other, they could do it," she reasoned. Genna promised them a family who would work, play, and pray together like normal families. That night, now more than a year ago, the kids agreed to try and trust Genna one more time.

Recovery is painful but possible. Keva is surprised by what she is learning about her mother. Divorced and head of the family, she is trying hard to make it all work. "She is a capable

Genna and Keva—mother and daughter coming to terms.

person," Keva says. At times, Genna's independence causes conflict, because Keva was in charge for so long. The family is no longer on welfare, because Genna is working and is a responsible employee. For Keva, it is vital that she free herself of guilt and understand that she is not the cause of her parents' drinking, anymore than Genna was responsible for her own parents' illness. Keva recognizes her own feelings now and can set realistic goals. She is establishing close relationships with peers and is no longer fearful of intimacy.

The children are like children everywhere who have frequent minor disagreements but are growing up healthy. With their mother, there are frequent renewals of vows of commitment to keep the new fragile family relationships intact. Keva is helped by her weekend and summer retreats with the support group Children of Alcoholics. She speaks to other teenagers in schools about her experience with drugs in hopes that kids may see the futility of drugging. At last, Keva feels beautiful. She is loved. She has a family. The drug connection of three generations is broken.

AGAINST GREAT ODDS

Some kids think that being the child of a minister or a cop is one of the worst things that can happen to someone. "Pressure is put on you to be the best behaved kid on the block, so you won't embarrass your folks," says Trevor. Tall, muscular but slim, Trevor looks fit enough to step into the ring. For the past year, daily workouts have helped to keep him in top condition. Trevor is 18 years old. He completed a one-year program of treatment at Outreach. He is working hard at a job he loves and making plans for the future, but there were times when his future looked bleak, especially since his alcoholic parents would not help him.

Trevor's parents divorced when he was nine years old. His father has remarried, but Trevor isn't too fond of his step-mother. Trevor's only sibling, a sister, moved out when she was eighteen years old. She has little contact with the family, who now live in a new house in a recently opened development.

Trevor's father has been a New York City police officer for nineteen years. He is proud to be one of New York's "finest." Trevor's stepmother is a legal aide in a Wall Street firm. "We have a good life," Trevor says. "But it's a phony life. We are very polite to each other. They don't tell me anything that I don't want to hear and I don't tell them anything they don't want to hear. This way we have no arguments. They really would like for me to leave and get my own place."

*M*ORE PHYSICAL THAN CEREBRAL

Trevor has always been a big, scrappy kid ready to decide all disagreements with his fists. At St. Gregory's elementary school, the nuns put Trevor's excess energy to work, having him beat erasers, wash blackboards, and clear tables in the cafeteria. Trevor enjoyed the attention and responsibility. The nuns recognized his limited ability and lack of interest in complex abstractions. When Trevor was in the fifth grade, he was still counting numbers with his fingers and reading at a third-grade level. But on the baseball field, he was a star. Trevor played center field. When Sister Brendon was at bat, Trevor braced himself for a long ball. She was fast too. Sister Brendon would round first base with her black veil flying straight out and her habit hitched up to her knees. Trevor's throw would be right on target, but Sister Brendon always slid right under the tag. When the umpire, Sister Ann, yelled, "Safe," Trevor threw up his arms in utter frustration. After each game, they would laugh about it and plan ways to get Sister Brendon at the next game.

*T*REVOR OPTS FOR CRACK

Trevor's problems began when he entered a large public high school. He felt lost amid the thousands of students. The work was difficult, the teachers too busy, and the students indifferent. In his sophomore year, Trevor became a truant. "I was failing anyway. I hated school." He joined a group of other dropouts who hung out in Murray Park. Almost anything could be bought there—especially stolen goods and drugs. Some kids there offered him angel dust, pot, and crack. And Trevor tried all of them. He spent more time with his new friends and crack than with anyone or anything else. When he was suspended from school, his father promised to provide stricter supervision. Trevor was reinstated, but things remained the same at home.

Trevor fell in love with crack and smoked it five to seven times a day. He dropped out of school and got a job. Although his salary was above average, it wasn't enough to support his growing habit. Trevor began to steal—anything from anyone. His parents, his friends, and eventually his employer became victims. Trevor stole money from his job and was fired. That same week, he was arrested for driving an expensive sports car. It was stolen. Trevor was crashing after smoking crack—and coming down hard. When his parents were called to the police station, they were amazed at his thinness, his haggard and drawn face and disheveled appearance. He looked like a dirty bum. They couldn't believe that he was an addict. But a search of Trevor's room confirmed it. His parents found pot, stolen credit cards, and his stepmother's gold jewelry hidden in a closet.

TREVOR HAS A CHOICE

Trevor's father was able to perform miracles. There would be no records. As a first offender, Trevor had a choice—"Go for treatment or do one-to-three," the judge said. Trevor chose treatment at Outreach. Trevor admits thinking that treatment would be a "piece of cake." "I'd just go there and they would work on me. I wouldn't have to do anything." Trevor didn't take orders easily. "I was tired of people telling me what to do. And I wanted to keep the memory of being high on crack alive. But most of all, I was scared." Seeing young men there hug each other, Trevor thought most of them were gay. So he kept to himself. Later he would learn that love has no gender preference.

He resisted change. Trevor liked being a "tough guy." But with all of the staff and residents showing him so much love and understanding, he found it increasingly difficult to maintain that image. Soon Trevor found himself participating in activities, volunteering, and making friends.

MAKING IT

Trevor thinks he owes his life to Outreach. "I used to hurt myself, cut myself, and punch brick walls. All because I wanted to punish this rotten guy. I like the new Trevor, who can assume responsibility and gets respect on the job." Trevor is making it without the interest or support of family. He doesn't feel anger or hatred toward them—just compassion. "I got through this. I can make it without them," Trevor says. Life can be miserable, but you can change it into what you want it to be, he thinks.

He earned his General Education Diploma and may go to college one day. He'd like to be a chef or a butcher. "Maybe someday I'll have my own restaurant!" he says.

He has this advice for other kids: "I always laughed at those drug education courses in school. Just some more crap to avoid. I believed that those things happened to other kids, not me. But it can happen to anyone. Don't be sucked into 'just trying it.' You're caught up with it before you know what happened."

Many kids, like Trevor, don't have the support or concern of family or even relatives. They have to go it alone. But they make it.

LIVING INSIDE OF A NIGHTMARE

It's Christmas Eve. And like Christmas Eve in most homes, there is last minute shopping to do, large odd-shaped packages to wrap and hide, tomorrow's dinner preparation to complete, and the tree to trim. But unlike most homes, the family in this home consists of 142 adults and 52 children. The family is called MABON (Mothers And Babies Off Narcotics) and is located on Ward's Island in New York City harbor. MABON is a residential treatment program for substance-addicted parents and their children conducted by Odyssey House, a well-known therapeutic community.

Kathy, an attractive, auburn-haired young woman, is a member of the tree-decorating committee. Tall, trim, and energetic, she looks like any one of the healthy joggers seen in the early mornings and evenings pacing herself along the East or Hudson Rivers. Kathy is hanging tinsel and silver bells on the upper branches. She hums "Santa Claus Is Coming to Town" as she works. She is excited and happy about the festivities planned for tomorrow. Responding to a sudden emotional urge, Kathy reaches down and hugs her young helpers—Sean and Cory, her sons. The exuberant children respond by pulling their mother off the stool for a wrestling roll on the floor. Kathy reaches under their bright blue sweaters and tickles their tummies. Their happy shrieks and squeals are matched by Kathy's hearty laughter. Tomorrow will be another milestone: her second drug-free Christmas.

As the kids run off to play, Kathy takes a breather. "It's painful to relive those times. My life before 'breaking the connection' was like living inside of a nightmare." Kathy sighs and looks at the floor. She is quiet for a long moment and finally looks up to say, "But telling it might help some kids to think twice before taking that first smoke, snort, or injection."

Kathy wishes she knew half of what she knows about drugs now. Here are a few of the things she learned:

1. The majority of kids do not use drugs.
2. Taking drugs is a personal, deliberate act.
3. Drugging keeps you from developing your intellect and skills and growing into a wonderful human being.
4. If you're thinking about starting, look around you: There are hundreds of options open to you.

5. Reach out to the many people who can offer information, guidance, and support and help you learn to cope with life.

DOUBLE LOSS

Kathy's childhood was uneventful and reasonably normal until one day, just after Kathy celebrated her sixth birthday, her mother left the house for a business appointment. Kathy's father was at work on his construction job, so her mother carefully locked Kathy and her twin sister in a bedroom for safety. Unfortunately, a fire broke out, and the apartment was partly destroyed. The children were not able to get out of the room. When the firefighters reached them, Kathy's sister was dead. The origin of the fire remains a mystery. Although no one accused her, Kathy felt guilty. Somehow, she should have been able to save her sister. From that day, Kathy's twin sister Margaret and her death were never mentioned by her parents. It was just as though she had never existed. Kathy missed Margaret, but she was afraid to even question her parents' silence.

After the funeral, Kathy's mother seemed to change. Kathy sensed a wall of silence between them. Within months, Kathy's mother suffered a mental breakdown and spent most of the next few years in bed. Kathy assumed responsibility for household chores and the care of two younger siblings. She felt that she had suffered a double loss—her identical twin and her mother. This feeling of loss remained with her throughout her adolescence.

TRICK, NOT TREAT

Kathy had a maternal aunt and uncle who lived in Nassau County, New York. Their suburban home was surrounded by flower gardens, open land, and woods. Each Sunday, Kathy and the younger children were invited to a "treat" in the country. After a week of school, hard work, and watching the children, Kathy looked forward to a carefree day. Her aunt's hospitality permitted Kathy's mother to have a quiet day without the children around the house too. This was her aunt's contribution to her sister's recovery.

On the pretense of gathering wild flowers and looking for birds' nests, Kathy's uncle always managed to get her away from the family group. They would go farther into the woods to look for a "special" bird. The bird never appeared, but for months, Kathy fought against her uncle's attempts to remove her clothes and touch her. She felt unable to tell anybody. Her uncle always bought expensive gifts for all of them, especially for Kathy. In any case, who could she tell? Her aunt would stop the Sunday outings and deny Kathy's mother her one day of rest. Kathy's father was an alcoholic and was rarely home, and he didn't talk to her very much anyway. Kathy believed that no one would listen to her. So she kept quiet about these fearful episodes.

These weekends came to a sudden stop when Kathy's uncle visciously raped her. In the hospital emergency room, Kathy protected everyone by claiming the blood and bruises were the result of a fall from a tree. The busy doctor knew better. But he didn't press her for a full explanation. Kathy felt more alone than ever now. She no longer had relatives she could trust. But even more, she was totally confused by the adults' cover up of the brutal sexual attack. When Kathy's mother was told, she turned away and refused to discuss it. Kathy, now 7 years old, had endured more pain than some adults experience in a lifetime. The incident seemed to validate Kathy's feelings of worthlessness and low self-esteem and convinced her that she caused trouble for everyone.

*R*OLE REVERSAL

Growing up with mounting responsibilities at home and at school can result in a lot of pressure and tension. It can be even more frustrating when there is no reward. Kathy's mother never resumed the care of the children, so by the age of nine Kathy had become "little mother." She cooked, shopped, washed, ironed, cleaned the apartment, and helped the younger children with their lessons. Kathy remained an excellent student, too. She not only loved learning, but school relieved her from domestic pressure for at least six hours a day. But because of her heavy schedule, she had few friends and rarely went out of the house.

It was Kathy's responsibility to keep the children quiet and out of her father's way when he came home from work. This assignment became critical if he had been drinking. But when he was sober, he loved to play with the young ones. He would roughhouse with them, tossing the children high in the air over his six-foot body. Kathy would hover nearby, fearful that their small arms or legs would be broken.

During these years, Kathy felt a growing resentment and anger toward her parents. Not only did she assume parental duties far beyond the capabilities of such a young person, but there was never any sign of appreciation or gratitude. All Kathy heard was more criticism for not doing more or doing it better. Kathy believed that she was the cause of her father's drinking. Perhaps if she did more and did it better, he would stop drinking. Many nights, she lay awake in bed trying to solve this puzzle.

Kathy was one of the youngest girls in her all-girl parochial high school. She was thirteen. In addition, she held a part-time job. Her brother and sisters were older now and able to assume some responsibility for their own care. Working made Kathy feel independent and kept her away from an unhappy home life. She was certain that her parents didn't love her. They never asked about the job or how and where she spent her time. Kathy found them cold, indifferent, and unreliable. She had no basic trust in them or any adults.

FIRST DATE

Kathy had her first date at sixteen. The relationship that developed lasted for two years. Kathy was not attracted to the young man because of his athletic talents or his good looks or appearance or any other positive characteristic. To the contrary, Kathy was grateful that someone, anyone, found her acceptable. She felt lucky to have his companionship. He needed someone to make him look good and Kathy was pretty and smart. There was little joy, deep feeling, or romance in their relationship.

Kathy transferred her affiliation from the family to her boyfriend. She spent the days in school and at work, but the evenings were devoted to "running the streets" with him, and hanging out in clubs, bars, and discos. After graduation, Kathy enrolled in the sophomore class of a local parochial college. She was seventeen years old. Because of her excellent grades and advanced work in high school, she was given credit for a year of college work. But she still felt rejected, inadequate, and lonely.

Although teenage pregnancy was happening all around her, Kathy never thought she might become a statistic. Perhaps if she had been emotionally involved with her boyfriend, becoming pregnant would have evoked feelings other than fear, guilt, and the notion that she had made another mistake. Kathy did not tell her parents until very late. She was afraid that they would throw her out. Kathy sensed that her mother knew about the pregnancy but chose to ignore it.

When she held her infant son, Kathy knew real happiness for the first time. She was somebody at last—a mother! A child of her own would mean that there would always be someone who needed and loved her.

Kathy's mother urged placement of the baby for adoption, saying Kathy was too young to take care of a child. This seemed contradictory, since Kathy had cared for her brother and sisters since she was six years old. She had also held part-time jobs and made the honor roll, so she knew she could take responsibility. Faced with these facts, Kathy's mother withdrew her objections. Surprisingly, Kathy's father agreed with his daughter. It was the first time he'd supported Kathy against his wife.

Before the baby's birth, Kathy had broken up with her boyfriend. Since their relationship was based upon Kathy's need to have someone care for her, Kathy felt the baby would more than fill that need.

To prove her capability, Kathy dropped out of school, found a small apartment, and worked 14 hours a day to support herself and the baby. From a teenage school girl, Kathy changed into a responsible, working adult overnight.

THE NEW LIFE AND COCAINE

Kathy's acquaintances were working class men and women employed in semiskilled jobs. Some of them used drugs, which were readily available in her neighborhood. Kathy feared drugs, because she had observed their effect on teenagers in the neighborhood. But she was lonely, tired, and often frustrated with her new role, and desperately wanted to be liked by her new friends. So she joined them in snorting cocaine.

In less than a year, Kathy had developed a two-hundred-dollar-a-day habit. She quit her job and went to work in a local nightclub, where cocaine was given to her by the owners. The club members and their friends were mostly coarse, boisterous, and ill-mannered men. Kathy hated their behavior, but was flattered because they found her attractive; she was accepted by them but not by herself.

It was during this low period that Kathy began a relationship with Ken. This young man's show of concern for Kathy's looks, future, and safety made her think that she had met "Mr. Right." She was so grateful for his attention that she willingly did everything and anything for him. Ken insisted that she leave the club; he found her an apartment in another section of the city, and got her off drugs. He even selected her clothes and makeup. For a while, Kathy was ecstatically happy. It took six months for Kathy to realize that he was as dependent on her as she was on him. He needed her gratitude to feel good about himself. Changing her made him feel creative, important, and worthwhile. But he did not welcome the news of her second pregnancy.

ON A COLLISION COURSE

At nineteen, Kathy had two small babies and one adult child—Ken. In addition, Ken was using cocaine and heroin. Kathy was mother to all three and worked two jobs to provide for the family. To please Ken, Kathy began to use cocaine again, and she turned to prostitution to earn money to buy it. Frequently, babysitters cared for the children while Kathy cruised bars and streets looking for customers. Ken was like a pimp. As soon as Kathy made a few dollars, he pocketed it. On those nights when Kathy's earnings were limited, Ken blamed himself. The next night he made sure that her makeup and clothes were "stand-outs." Getting high and worrying about money to get drugs became Kathy and Ken's total preoccupation. The youngsters were often neglected as drugs took priority over child care.

One night Kathy picked up a man in a Manhattan bar. He took her to a house in Queens. He was joined by four friends who ripped off Kathy's clothes and tied her to a bed. Kathy was repeatedly raped and abused by these four men for three days. She was not fed, and she was untied only to relieve herself in a pail kept in a corner of the room. The men had all kinds of drugs, and Kathy begged for something, anything, to help her become unconscious. But they refused her pleas. The physical pain was severe, and being treated worse than a trapped animal was emotionally devastating. Kathy prayed for death.

At the end of the third day a fifth man, who had been an observer during the entire ordeal, untied her. She thought she was about to die. Quivering with fear and cold, she mumbled prayers vaguely remembered from her childhood. To her surprise, the man opened a window, pointed to her torn clothing, and left the room. Kathy quickly dressed in what was left of her blouse, bra and skirt. Her shoes and other clothing were nowhere in sight. She climbed down the rusty fire escape, cutting her feet in several places. Once on the ground, she was too weak and dizzy to run. Kathy walked about seven or eight blocks in the strange neighborhood, until she saw a shopping mall. She noticed a car in the parking lot with M.D. plates and collapsed against it. When the doctor returned with her packages, she looked at Kathy with suspicion and disbelief. She insisted that the police be called, but Kathy was determined that they not be notified. The doctor wanted to drive Kathy to the nearest hospital, but Kathy refused this offer too. All she wanted was to see her children. For three days, she had kept her hopes alive with thoughts of being with the babies again. The doctor reluctantly agreed to drive Kathy to the babysitter's house, five miles away. The kind woman gently wrapped Kathy's bleeding feet in a towel and gave her a sweater to keep her warm. Kathy thanked her and promised to get medical help later.

The babysitter was not glad to see Kathy. She had not been paid. Since she had not heard from Kathy for three days, she had considered the children abandoned. The police had taken the children and turned them over to the child-care authorities. They were now in foster homes.

NOTHING LEFT

With little hope of ever getting her children back, because she had been declared an unfit mother by the social service agency, Kathy felt she had no reason to go on living. She had never realized how much the boys really meant to her. Ken discarded Kathy like a scrap of garbage, since she no longer filled his needs. He gave away her clothes and sold the furniture for drugs. The only place left for her was the streets. Prostitution for money or drugs in cars, doorways, motels, and parking lots became Kathy's life. There were times when she didn't get paid or get the promised drugs, or worse, the drugs were diluted. But Kathy didn't care anymore. She felt that she deserved this kind of treatment as punishment for all the wrong things committed in her past. She didn't feel worthy of anything better. Twice she deliberately tried to overdose. When she awoke in the hospital, she became hysterical at her failure.

At this point, Kathy was incapable of performing normal, daily self-care. She remembers spending six days in a nightclub without a bath or change of clothes. Kathy overheard some of her recent male customers discussing her in an extremely uncomplimentary manner. She despised herself. She felt like a stray animal that belonged to no one.

Instead of taking more drugs to ease the pain, she thought of her children and her family. She was tired of her life. She wanted something better for herself. "If I don't have what it takes to kill myself, maybe I can get the strength to pull myself together," Kathy reasoned. Several years earlier, Kathy's family had urged her to seek help for her drug habit. She had consented in order to stop their nagging, but only stayed in the center for two months. Getting unhooked now would be difficult, but Kathy was finding it more difficult to stay alive on the streets. She wanted her children, but even more she wanted life. Kathy decided the time had come to break the connection.

*G*ETTING UNHOOKED

Unfortunately, Kathy reached bottom before asking for help. When she arrived at Odyssey House, only 86 pounds covered her 5-foot, 6-inch frame. She was frightened and had little grasp of reality. But whatever the program offered, Kathy knew it couldn't be any worse than what she was enduring on the streets. Kathy now believes that there are several steps you must take in order for the treatment to work. First, you must admit that you need help to break the connection. Second, you must be willing to help yourself. The last is most painful, but you must examine what happened, why it happened, and what you contributed to the situation. In a therapeutic community, such openness is possible because more of the residents and some of the counselors have experienced firsthand the horrible life of an addict. They surround the newcomer with care and understanding. They become a surrogate family. Within this family group are some who have graduated from Odyssey's program. Knowing they were able to make changes in their lives gives the resident hope.

THERAPY LEADS TO UNDERSTANDING

Kathy recalls her early life as being normal until the death of her identical twin. She realizes now that what she interpreted as indifference and rejection by her mother was her mother's way of dealing with her own guilt and pain. Kathy was a constant reminder of the other child, who had died as a result of a mother's good intentions but poor judgment. Lack of parental reliability deepened Kathy's sense of isolation. She never developed strong emotional ties with either parent. Very early, Kathy learned that most adults, including parents and other relatives, are not to be believed or trusted. Not receiving any help or support after the rape, her rage left deep emotional scars that still have not healed.

Children of alcoholics learn early that the use of alcohol and other drugs is a way to cope with tension. With all the verbal and psychological abuse in the home, Kathy first sought escape through positive avenues of academic achievement and employment. But that didn't fulfill her basic needs for love, acceptance, approval, and worth, or diminish inner turmoil. She was easy prey for anything that could possibly fulfill these needs, including drugs or alcohol. Kids who do drugs often talk about having such feelings of low self-esteem.

As the oldest child of an alcoholic father and a mother unable to cope with her family's needs, role changes in the family were inevitable. Kathy was forced to grow up prematurely and become mother to her younger siblings. Playing several roles increased confusion for her: she was surrogate mother, a daughter in need of guidance and supervision, and a growing child missing the emotional support and friendship of peers. She felt unwanted by both parents and naturally experienced anger, frustration, and hostility toward them. Because of their own insecurity, egocentricity, and capriciousness, Kathy's parents were poor role models.

Kathy now believes one close friend, adult or child, would have provided an outlet for her need to communicate the confusion caused by these ever-changing roles.

THE NEW KATHY

Kathy knows that you can learn how to feel better about yourself, but you must work at it constantly. All the things you need to get unhooked are already within you. It's Kathy herself, not the drugs, that controls her life. She has learned to trust others and form positive relationships with people. Having her two sons with her has strengthened Kathy's determination to create a warm, loving family. She is learning how to be a parent again, and helping the boys overcome the emotional trauma of living in a series of foster-care homes. Kathy finds joy in watching the children grow and develop. The happiness she feels is hard for her to describe. But watching Kathy romp with her active, healthy sons beneath the Christmas tree tells it all. "I love myself. I love my life. I am content!" she says softly. A job, college, good health, positive attitudes, and the ability to cope are only a few of the positive features in Kathy's future.

Some day, Kathy hopes that she can become reconciled with her parents, brother, and sisters. They all missed so much, living and growing up in such a tense environment.

During treatment, a great deal of time is spent dealing with past anger, hostility, and hate and trying to put them into perspective. Residents of Odyssey House programs call it "picking up the pieces and putting them back together again." But in spite of all the tragedy, there were some good times, and Kathy would like her mother to know they are remembered. Here is a letter that she sent to her mother recently.

> *Dear Momma:*
>
> *If you could see me now, you would feel real proud of the changes I've made. I am a good mother to your two wonderful grandsons. My life is full of surprises, and I discover new and different strengths each day.*
>
> *At night, when the children are asleep, I think about those times when we were a family. Do you remember the time I danced in the school's Irish Dance Festival? I had a special costume and danced without missing a step. When I spotted you and Dad smiling*

Kathy, healthy and happy, with her prized possessions.

at me from the audience, I was so happy. Later we went on some of the rides, and you both told me how proud you felt seeing me perform.

Another good time was a picnic in the state park. After we broiled the frankfurters and hamburgers, little Jimmie wandered off into the woods. We were all so frightened, because he was only three years old. Everyone ran in all directions looking for him. But I found him! That made me feel good. Afterward, we celebrated with ice cream and cake with lots of hugs and kisses.

You probably don't recall my most favorite toy. It was a special doll you gave me one Christmas. The one that had a record in the back? When you wound it up, you could have a conversation with the doll. I was the only kid in the apartment house who had one. I loved it and you for making me so special.

There was another good time when you came to high school's Gymnastic Contest. You surprised me, because I hadn't told you about the performance or that I was competing. I didn't think you would even be interested or care. Boy was I surprised! There you were grinning from ear to ear when they announced my name as the winner of the parallel bar competition. I wonder whatever happened to that medal?

It's been helpful for me to just remember some of the happy times. Thanks.

Love,

Kathy

VICTOR MEANS WINNER!

Victor means winner, but, to one young man, it once meant victim. His full name is Victor Fuentes, and he is a Newrican—which means that he was born stateside of Puerto Rican parents.

Baby Victor was delivered by a police officer eighteen years ago in an abandoned car on East 118th Street, New York. When Victor was three years old, his father, a mechanic, left the family of four boys with their mother. "He just went to work one day and didn't come back," says Victor.

ALCOHOL—THE POPULAR DRUG

Raising four active boys in a crowded five-room apartment in Taft Houses was not easy for Mrs. Fuentes. Situated in the heart of East Harlem's El Barrio, Taft Houses played a major part in the area's drug traffic. But growing up, Victor was more aware of alcohol as being a popular drug. Most of the men in the housing project seemed to drink alcoholic beverages a lot. They slept off their drunken stupors on the benches in the courtyard, urinated in the hallways, and vomited in the elevators.

At thirteen, Victor was re-introduced to his father. Victor smelled alcohol and noticed the unsteady gait. "He was just like those guys on the benches," the disappointed youth recalled. Victor disliked the older man immediately. Mrs. Fuentes was a factory worker and often worked overtime to support the boys. After school, Victor and his older brother cared for their two younger brothers. They prepared dinner, fed them and played with the boys until Mrs. Fuentes came home. Later on, Victor would remember these times as the happiest in his young life.

NIGHT LIFE

At night, Victor and his older brother joined their friends on the streets and made the rounds, stopping in bars, clubs, and pool rooms. "There were six of us, and we called ourselves 'Spidermen.' That's because we reached into everything—bins and shelves in stores, people's pockets, wallets, purses, and windows." All six youths wore expensive black leather jackets with a colorful spider emblazoned on the backs. At night, the sight, sounds, and smells of the streets were intensified. Salsa music was louder and wilder, odors of garlic and other spices and herbs were stronger, and the clothes of the colorfully costumed strollers competed with blazing, flickering neon signs. Drug dealers and pushers slouched against darkened doorways. Victor and his friends bought pot, mescaline, and cocaine easily, despite their obvious youth. "Once we started to get high," says Victor, "we jumped the turnstiles in the subway."

The Spidermen terrorized passengers on the subway trains with threatening gestures, screams, and stares. "We grabbed gold chains, pocketbooks, radios, cassette players, and watches. We tried not to hurt people, but sometimes they got knocked off their feet." The boys also vandalized the subways. If they were really out of control, they shattered windows and ripped seats with their knives. The transit cops chased them frequently, but the next night the Spidermen were back on the trains—except once, when the cops escorted them to the street at the last subway stop. The boys found themselves in another county with no money. By the time the youths walked several miles to the next station, the rowdy Spidermen were more like meek lambs.

Dropping Out

Spending most of the night in the streets and subways left little time for sleep. So Victor slept in most of his classes at Carver Junior High School. He lost or misplaced most of his books. This was his excuse for falling behind in required homework. The teachers took little notice of the sleeping student and were possibly grateful that he was quiet. Victor liked Physical Education and was present in that class about 90 percent of the time. He liked to play ball, learn karate, and swim. After the class, he left school.

Meanwhile Victor's drug use was escalating. He now drank whiskey during the day as well as at night. As his need for drugs increased, Victor had to find new sources of money to pay for his addiction. He began by stealing the family's television set, table radio, and video cassette recorder. The police recovered the items for his mother, but she was hurt and angry with Victor and determined to get him off drugs.

Mrs. Fuentes belonged to a Pentecostal church. None of the boys ever joined her in celebrations of the rituals and practices of the church. Victor, particularly, called them phony. However, Mrs. Fuentes decided to try exorcism to rid Victor of the devil who had gained control of his body and soul. At first, she merely sprinkled "holy water" around Victor's empty bed and knelt there for long periods chanting softly. After three months, she realized that nothing was going to happen.

Early one morning, about 4:00 A.M., Victor was awakened by holy water being poured over his face by a tall, angular man dressed in black. In the glowing, soft candlelight, his grotesque features looked like those of a gargoyle. The odor of acrid and pungent incense filled the small room. The man bellowed "Let him out," as he swung a heavy carving knife over Victor's body. With one giant leap, Victor cleared the bed and ran toward the door, opened it, and sped down the stairs wearing only a thin, tattered undershirt. Mrs. Fuentes stood by the open apartment door begging Victor to come back. He didn't. After a long sleep at a friend's house, he decided to leave home. He was sixteen years old, a truant with several juvenile citations issued by the police, and he was afraid that his mother would succeed in placing him in an institution for delinquent boys. To get enough money to buy food and drugs, Victor robbed small groceries and other stores in the bordering neighborhoods of Harlem and the East Bronx. Frequently he "cased" the stores during the day and broke in at night.

*T*URNING POINT

Victor continued to spend his days and nights in an alcoholic, cocaine-laced stupor. At times, his brother gave him money. Reluctantly, he accepted money from his alcoholic father. Victor lost weight, his health, and his friends. The other Spidermen were gone . . . either dead from overdosing or incarcerated in Rikers Island prison. Victor seemed to be losing out everywhere too. "All I had was drugs, and they were killing me." Victor felt like a victim of himself.

At Outreach, Victor found many people who were instrumental in changing the attitude of the former swaggering tough guy. "The hardest part was taking a good look at myself. I stunk," he remembers. It was difficult learning how to trust peers and adults. But group work taught Victor that it was possible, particularly when the group convinced him of his great potential. "They recognized good things in me. That made me feel like I was a real person with worth."

VICTOR'S ASSESSMENT

"I think that I played the most important role in my treatment. I did it for myself," Victor says proudly. "I care about myself. I want to grow and love people. And I need people to help me."

Victor is a winner. He is back in high school studying a beginning computer science course, which he enjoys. Community college and a part-time job are his goals after June 1987 graduation. Victor doesn't miss the old neighborhood or its fake dreams. He's found a healthier place that can't be defined geographically but is with him always.

4
A STITCH
IN TIME

"Going it alone" is one of America's greatest myths; it rejects the reality that strength, growth, and accomplishment come through the support of communities . . . and communities mean people. Father Terrence Attridge, Director of the Substance Abuse Ministry Training Program of the Archdiocese of New York, says, "The 'quick fix' of substance abuse seems to be an attractive alternative to the 'long haul' of nurturing self-confidence and self-respect. All youth live in the present."

The real challenge for those who influence young people is to support them "here and now" so they can move with confidence toward fulfilling their potential. Adults and teenagers themselves should recognize the talents and gifts of young people and help them to develop and discover more of these abilities in their lives. The "significant adults" in the lives of young people—adults who are models for daily living—can help them reach their potential by supporting them through the "long haul" with patience, humor, and compassion.

This chapter will review some of the ways in which adults help youths with "a stitch in time" . . . in time to prevent the "quick fix" detour on the road to personal development.

YOUNG PEOPLE HELPING EACH OTHER

All across the country, trained "peer counselors" are helping other young people express feelings, explore options, and reach decisions. Increasingly, these decisions involve pregnancy, suicide, drug abuse, anxiety about tests, loneliness, divorce in families, and dropping out of school. The counselors lead courses in schools like Cranford High School in New Jersey. Michael Blasucci, vice principal, helped organize the program as part of the freshman health curriculum. There are thirty classes, which are conducted by forty-eight counselors who are juniors and seniors. Faculty members meet with leaders regularly and may drop into classes unannounced occasionally. But otherwise, the teenagers run the show. "To get true peer communication, you can't have us old fuddy-duddies around," says the vice principal.

Although peer counselors at Cranford receive intensive training in communication and curriculum topics, they are not experts and are required to alert program advisers to life-threatening situations. The youngsters listen with a "third" ear and can pick up on "heavy" stuff. If a student does not feel comfortable in a class situation, a peer counselor will meet that student in the cafeteria, locker room, or library and start a conversation. "You would be surprised how receptive even the coolest kid can be to a little caring," a seventeen-year old senior reported.

The focus of peer projects varies. Here are some examples:

- In Tyonek, Alaska, a tiny village where eight of thirty teenagers have taken their lives in recent years, peer counselors work with children as young as eight to combat suicide and drug abuse.
- In Perior, Illinois, mental health workers have trained teenagers to operate a crisis telephone line for other teenagers who call in anonymously.

A Peer Class for freshmen meets at Cranford High School, New Jersey.

- In San Francisco, "small-conflict managers" in grades four through six are credited with breaking up scuffles and lunch-money extortion rings.
- In New York City, six high schools are part of Project Smart. The name is an acronym for School Mediations Alternative Resolution Team. At Taft High School, one of the schools involved, there are thirty-two peer mediators. They encourage students to submit arguments and disputes to mediation. At times, it may take several meetings of negotiations before a contract is signed by both parties. Youths shake hands and agree to bury the hatchet. The mediators, in addition to settling disputes, discourage drug traffic in and outside the building, spot students who appear lonely, orient new students, and patrol areas where students hang out.

In some schools, young counselors wear distinctive T-shirts or armbands identifying them as counselors or conflict managers. In several programs, the counselors are elected solely by peers; in others by panels of peers and faculty. The most effective programs draw counselors from every clique in the school, not just the kids with an A average. "You need jocks, preppies, nerds, wimps, groupies, and punks," a Florida freshman says. "You need your leather jackets too," a sophomore added.

"It's between me and you," each client is told. Except for life-or-death situations like potential suicides, peer counselors must promise not to divulge confidences. In one Los Angeles high school counseling office, there is a sign that reads: WHAT YOU HEAR HERE, WHAT YOU SAY HERE, WHEN YOU LEAVE HERE, STAYS HERE.

In schools where peer counselors and mediators are carefully trained and supervised, the results are encouraging. "There is some evidence they help reduce violence and discipline problems and are well accepted by other kids," said Dr. Morton Deutsch, a social psychologist at Teachers College of Columbia University.

At Paul Revere School in San Francisco, a playground dispute is settled through mediation.

BOYS HARBOR

Born with a silver spoon in his mouth in a house on the right side of the railroad tracks, Anthony Drexel Duke takes social responsibility very seriously. He is the driving force behind Boys Harbor. For more than fifty years, this scion of wealth and high social class has devoted his life to improving the condition of underprivileged kids from depressed areas of New York City. Duke has used his financial and social resources to help more than 2,500 inner-city kids who attend a year-round preschool, after-school, and summer program.

Duke's concern for underprivileged kids began in 1934 when he took a job at his prep-school's welfare camp. His first project was to set up a summer camp for youngsters whose families had been victims of the severe economic depression of the 1930s. The camp was forced to close during World War II, but in 1950 it was reopened on 180 acres of land in Nassau County, New York. All of Duke's own eleven children have grown up at the camp, and some of the older ones have worked as counselors there.

Like the other Boys Harbor projects, the summer camp offers a variety of educational and sports activities, encouraging kids to enjoy and exploit their particular strengths. Self-respect is emphasized in the camp's programs, and those who join are screened for adaptability. Parents who can afford it are asked to pay a small fee.

At 8:00 A.M. every morning, more than fifty preschool children arrive at Boys Harbor's large gray building on the East Side of Manhattan. These youngsters are from hotels for the homeless. They will be given breakfast and lunch and take part in play activities geared to strengthening language, coordination and creative experiences. "We emphasize critical thinking, because if you can think, you can do anything," the executive director, a former camp counselor, believes.

When regular school is over, neighborhood kids hurry to Boys Harbor for classes in art, science, drama, mathematics, computers, philosophy, and law. Swimming, basketball, dance,

"I didn't think I'd be up so high." Kids ride high in the saddle at
Boys Harbor Camp.

and music lessons are available too. Older teens may use the gymnasium and pool until late in the evening. The program's success has created a long waiting list of kids wishing to join. "But we make it clear," says Duke, "that they must use the tools we offer. We look for results—academic improvement, behavior patterns—all the things you would look for in your own children." Duke is proud of the kids who have graduated from Boys Harbor programs, and now occupy every walk of life.

The Harbor offers a comprehensive program of drug education. Professional counselors train teenage groups to visit schools in their own neighborhoods and talk with students. These peer counselors conduct small group discussions and set up "role-playing" exercises. Many of the students come from homes where alcohol is abused by one or both parents. The peer counselors try to help students understand what happens when you live in such a household. They learn how alcohol has an impact on family members. They also learn that *they* are not responsible for their parents' drinking. The peers teach coping skills and discuss alternatives to alcohol and other drugs. The response from the children is immediate and relevant. They are helped to understand the values of abstinence and self-discipline, despite the drug-infested environment that often surrounds them.

Over the past five or six years, girls have become a part of the exciting programs offered at the Harbor. The agency has continued to upgrade its programs in drug education and prevention, values training, and sex and health education.

Duke is working to insure the future of the Harbor with an endowment of $10 million, so the spirit and programs will continue after the Dukes are no longer running it. "I've always worried," he said to a *New York Times* reporter in November 1986, "what would happen to our country if too many people slipped out of the system? Too many human resources are not being used and people are being left out of the dream. We've found that children on the street have a dream. They reach out for whatever we can give."

"❚ HAVE A DREAM PROGRAM"

Pedro Rivera, Juan Melendez, and Maria Valdes never expected to meet a millionaire—especially in East Harlem. But seven years ago, one came to their sixth-grade graduation at P.S. 121 in Manhattan. His name was Eugene Lang, and he too graduated from P.S. 121, about fifty years ago.

Pedro, Juan, and Maria remember the hot June day, the warm auditorium and uncomfortable hard seats. As the white, middle-aged man walked to the podium, the kids prepared themselves for the boring speech they thought they were about to hear. Their mothers' fanning picked up momentum, and their fathers loosened ties around the scratchy collars of new white shirts. "I thought about taking a nap," Maria recalls. "Then people began to mumble, cry out, and then applaud. I didn't know what was happening."

What happened was Lang put away his "graduation speech" and spoke from his heart. "I promise," he said slowly, "to guarantee each of today's sixty-one graduates a college education." Everyone was excited. Was it some kind of joke? They had heard so many promises from public officials, landlords, and politicians. "It just seemed unreal," Pedro said. The auditorium was in an uproar. People jumped out of their seats.

When everyone calmed down, Lang disclosed his plan. Every year, he would set aside two thousand dollars for each graduate's future college tuition. Later he said, "I wanted to give them hope and reasonable expectation. If they work sincerely in school and apply themselves to fulfilling their dreams, then those dreams become possible. Giving them money was only a means of inspiring them to work toward their goals." With these words, the "I Have a Dream Program" was born.

Giving money was the easiest part. Lang is a very busy man. Among his many ventures is the Refac Technology Development Corporation, which he owns. He is a trustee of the New School for Social Research and a member of boards at other institutions of higher education. But he still finds time for his "family" of students. They visit him in his office and he shares the highs and lows of their lives. They go camping and enjoy other social activities with him.

Lang realized that money was only part of what was needed. The kids could not make it without other kinds of support. So he provided tutorial help, especially in English, social sciences, mathematics, and the sciences. He arranged individual tutoring at Harlem's Youth Action Program. Preparation for the SAT (Scholastic Aptitude Test) was also made available to the kids. A young Hispanic counselor was hired to coordinate support services for the students and their families. The counselor, John Rivera, keeps the lines of communication open twenty-four hours a day. The kids feel that he is part of their extended family.

After their sixth-grade graduation, the group was dispersed among twenty different junior and senior high schools. Weekly telephone calls, meetings, outings and recreational activities kept the group feeling alive. The kids cheered each other's successes and provided comfort and understanding when their peers made slip-ups.

For most of these kids, there is little in their surroundings to encourage success at school. Some of the black and Hispanic inner-city kids attend schools where the dropout rate is more than 50 percent. Police report drug-related crime in the area as being the second highest in New York City. Drug use and abuse are equally high. Heroes tend to be drug dealers, number runners, gamblers, hustlers, and petty thieves.

Despite peer pressure, the jibes of other kids, poverty and decaying housing, and poor role models in the kids' neighborhood, the program has been a success. In June 1987, fifty-two of the original group will graduate from high school. Most will go on to good colleges around the country. One has chosen a career in the Armed Services. And several others want work experience. But Lang is not disappointed. "The object, of course, is to get these kids into college if that is what they want. But what really matters is that the program provides an alternative to crime and drugs and gives the kids a chance to choose what they'll do with their lives," he says.

Mr. Lang celebrates with his kids in the "I Have a Dream Program."

The kids speak happily of parental support, teacher interest, and the cohesiveness of the group. Aristides Alvarado says, "Mr. Lang was inspired by Martin Luther King's "I Have a Dream" speech and wanted us to have a dream too. The program gave me something to look forward to, something worth waiting for. It is a golden feeling." Another student, William Nazario, speaks warmly of Lang. "I think Mr. Lang just emits love. I don't think of him as a millionaire anymore. I think of him as a millionaire at heart." The enthusiasm of the group is obvious. "We don't want to let Mr. Lang or the other kids down. But more important, we don't want to let ourselves down," say Pedro, Juan, and Maria.

Some of the best news is that Lang's efforts are being duplicated as other benefactors choose to become guardian angels to kids in depressed areas of New York City. Nine new benefactors have promised college "dreams" to about 520 sixth graders around the city. These wealthy business executives will carry out Lang's ideas and practices as closely as possible. Each will adopt an entire class, steer them through junior and senior high school, and help them get admitted to college, if that is their wish. Like the parents of Lang's first group, the new ones find the offer diffcult to accept. "It's not just the money. It's the idea that someone, a total stranger, cares and is willing to help," one father said.

The word spread beyond New York City; and soon Dallas, Texas, had an "I Have a Dream Program" for more than one thousand children. Lang personally helped initiate the program for "high-risk kids" living in poverty- and crime-ridden areas. "I don't like to see a bridle put on the human spirit," said the self-made millionaire. "A view that one 'can't afford college so why try' is a bridle."

In addition to Dallas, twenty other cities are ready to start programs of their own. Lang has demonstrated that kids can have a brighter future, in spite of long odds, when people commit themselves to personal involvement in saving their lives.

THE DANCE THEATRE OF HARLEM

It's auditions day. The dressing room is crowded with girls and boys anxiously waiting to hear their names called. Some practice, some exercise and stretch their bodies, some bite their nails, and others are trying to hold back tears. The brave ones look around and try to guess who will be the lucky ones . . . only twenty out of one hundred will be chosen. The lucky ones will become members of the Workshop Ensemble who perform for community organizations and schools throughout metropolitan New York City. However, for those not selected, there are opportunities to demonstrate their talents, because the Dance Theatre of Harlem welcomes everyone, with or without extraordinary talent.

The Dance Theatre of Harlem School stands in the first ranks of the world's great ballet schools, and is both an accredited dance-training institution and an active communication center. Its mission remains the same as it was when it was founded in 1969: to offer students, especially those who are culturally and financially deprived, the opportunity to study and excel in dance and other related arts, and through that study to gain discipline and creativity that will serve them in all walks of life.

"We try to reach them early," says an instructor . . . "even before they know the meaning of pot, beer, whiskey, or crack." The Community Service Program serves this purpose by offering predance classes for children three to eight years old. The school occupies a renovated three-studio building in Central Harlem, very accessible to New York's public transportation system. Easy access permits children from different parts of the city to attend.

Dancing requires good health, positive attitudes, proper nutrition, discipline, and stamina. "All of these are built into our Childrens' Pre-Professional Program, which offers children eight to fifteen a rigorous introduction to ballet techniques. Recently, a special boys' ballet class was opened for boys under the age of twelve. The Teenage Pre-Professional Program offers

Healthy bodies and minds coupled with discipline and hard work make these young people the pride of The Dance Theatre of Harlem.

students ages thirteen and up more intensive ballet instruction plus tap dance classes. Scholarships play a very important role, since many of the talented students discovered in auditions simply do not have the means to pay tuition or living expenses. The students are proud to be drug-free, despite what they see going on around them. A dancer needs a positive self-image in order to project his or her God-given talent. Then he or she can really say, 'Look Ma I'm dancing.' "

GIRL SCOUTS

In 1987, the Girl Scouts celebrated their seventy-fifth anniversary. They will also celebrate more than 50 million women who got a head start on their futures through Girl Scouting. Everyone knows about their cookies and camping, but these young women do much more. Here are some examples of contemporary scouting:

- Juniors, Cadettes, and Seniors used their print-making skills to create Halloween cards and masks for children at St. Mary's Hospital in New York City. They later staged a play with puppets made from cereal box tops.
- Girls Scouts were among the hundreds of volunteers who handed out cups of water to thirsty runners in the New York City Marathon in 1986.
- A troop from Staten Island, New York, made and donated a Gingerbread Village to a neighborhood hospital's pediatric ward.
- Other troops planted and maintained flower gardens around senior citizen housing.
- Scouts helped in voter registration and food distribution programs throughout New York City.

But the highlight of 1986 for New York's Girl Scouts was a "Free to Be Me" weekend at a campsite in Dutchess county. In addition to recreational activities and sports, the scouts focused on these topics: teenage pregnancy, suicide, and drug preven-

Girl Scouts enjoy two-person canoe racing.

tion. Adult leaders assisted peer groups in discussion, role playing and counseling. The nine- to fifteen-year-olds created posters, puppets, and songs in keeping with the theme. They also came up with ways to make some of the program's features year-round activities. "Each person has a choice, a decision to make as to how she will live. Drug-free is best," said a twelve-year-old.

Merit badges have always been a sign of youth achievement in learning. They come from participating in a program, demonstrating a skill, and contributing to the community. So it is no surprise that the Girl Scouts of Westchester/Putnam have a program that leads to a special Alcohol/Dependency Awareness Patch (ACDAP). Through this educational course developed with Drug Alcohol Rehabilitation Education (DARE), the National Council on Alcoholism of Westchester, and other agencies, girls receive recognition for developing their awareness of substance abuse. Their training covers the economic toll on society as well the enormous personal anxiety that drug and alcohol abusers and their families face. The program is aimed at preventing the scouts themselves from courting substance abuse, at giving them a strong basis for making wise choices, and at making them a healthy influence on their friends.

This innovative program is the first of its kind in New York State. More than 200 Girl Scouts and Brownies from Westchester/Putnam received their patches from New York governor Mario Cuomo in 1986.

*B*OY SCOUTS

Throughout its history, Boy Scouts of America has stood for principles that have encouraged youth to seek positive life values. Explorers, who are teenage scouts, are trained in the identification, use, misuse, and effects of drugs. The young people assist with drug awareness programs conducted in their communities and in their schools. These programs are oriented toward why young people use drugs, how to say no, and alternatives to drug use. Scout organizations are encouraged to adapt programs to suit their local needs. A full range of audio-visual materials is available to supplement activities.

Among the programs available are "Drugs: A Deadly Game," intended to make Cubs, Scouts, Explorers, and their leaders aware of the size of the drug problem in America; "Youth to Youth," which teaches youngsters that it is okay not to get involved in drug use; and "Teen Involvement," which aims to prevent substance abuse by encouraging positive communication between teenagers.

All Explorers are urged to work with church, recreational, and social agencies as well as with individuals and groups under the supervision of teachers and guidance counselors in their schools.

*Y*OUTH AT RISK PROGRAM

Labeled an "active-intervention program," Youth at Risk stresses that disadvantaged youths do not have to victimize others or become victims themselves to survive. The program also emphasizes that they have the power to control and change their lives.

"The system is not working for these kids, who usually end up as dropouts or in jail," says Chaya Deyo, program coordinator. "This program offers another way to reach the kids. They become responsible for themselves and others. They start to trust adults. The kids begin to use their support systems. We have all cultures, all ages, all backgrounds coming together."

The program is staffed and managed by volunteers selected from among teachers and the staffs of other community organizations. The youngsters joining Youth at Risk are from fifteen to twenty years old, and are referred by New York City's Probation Department, city youth agencies, and schools. The program, which runs for two years, offers the youths health and job counseling, physical exercise, confidence-building projects, and a strenuous ten-day course at a campsite in either Massachusetts or upstate New York.

At the ten-day course, an endurance test on ropes teaches

A counselor cheers a youngster as he climbs to the top of a tree in the "Youth at Risk" program in Massachusetts.

cooperation and teamwork. Another exercise puts the youngsters against a 15-foot wooden wall with no hand- or footholds. The group must act together to get everybody over.

The program's greatest strengths are in teaching values, commitment, and morals. Kimberly Rock, a city probation officer and former volunteer, believes the program gives the youths role models other than pimps and crack dealers. "Programs like this have to be considered part of the solution in helping kids keep out of the drug scene," says Rock. Some kids go to the program expecting to be victimized, because they are minority youths. They don't expect much from society. They have been in situations where promises are made and not fulfilled.

"They live in communities where they are exposed to everything. They think they can profit from breaking the law. When they go into the program, they are shocked that the people care."

THE CHILDREN'S MUSEUM OF MANHATTAN

Imagine a place so uniquely designed for children that it opens the door to a world full of creative possibilities and endless hours of participatory fun. The Children's Museum of Manhattan, the first and only museum for children in New York City, helps children learn about the environment in which they live while discovering their own creativity. Children have the opportunity to participate in art and science activities both in the museum itself, and through a range of community programs. The museum provides opportunities for young and old, affluent and disadvantaged alike.

One of the programs at the museum is an internship for high-risk high school students that was launched by the A. L. Mailman Family Foundation. The young people who take part have considered dropping out of school. Many are doing passing work in school, but find it too routine, too boring, and not relevant to what they want to do with their lives.

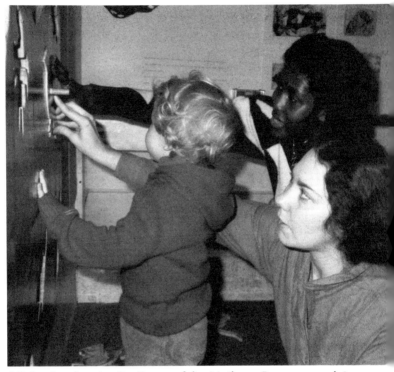

*High school senior Pat Facey of the Mailman Program explains
an educational exercise to a mother and her child at The
Children's Museum of New York City.*

The program permits the students to work with staff, artists, technicians, video experts, and child development researchers in a most exciting way. The interns become a part of the musuem staff. Twenty-five girls and boys from five high schools in Manhattan are given the opportunity to express themselves better through nontraditional, creative means, be it art, media, or interest in working with children.

In addition to attending technical training and assistance workshops, interns spend time in exhibit design and construction; graphics and fine arts techniques; administrative and secretarial skills; public relations and advertising; and art education and teaching. The students create their own projects, write journals, and attend in-house staff development seminars on aesthetics, education, and museum management. From January to June they visit corporations and businesses related to the communication field.

The coordinator, Carol Ashcraft, finds the students completely turned on in this unique environment. "No one has dropped out of the program or school. They don't have time for drugs," she says.

THE BOYS CHOIR OF HARLEM

If you've never been more than fifty blocks from your tenement apartment and never traveled in an airplane, the culture shock of visiting a foreign country can be quite an emotional experience. "I tried walking in those wooden shoes. How do they do it?" Ronald wondered. Meeting real kings and princes was almost as terrifying for Justin. "I thought they were only in stories," he says. Similar comments were made by the boys after visits to Norway, Germany, England, and France. The boys are members of the Boys Choir of Harlem.

The Boys Choir of Harlem was founded in 1968. The choir offers a comprehensive program of music education, counseling, tutoring, and recreational activities for inner-city children aged nine to seventeen. In the past eleven years, the choir has grown to become one of the finest boys choirs in the country

The Boys Choir of Harlem performs at the 1986 Centennial of the Statue of Liberty.

today. The boys have performed before audiences in colleges, churches, and community centers, as well as in major performance centers like Carnegie Hall, Radio City Music Hall, and Alice Tully Hall. The choir has made four tours in the United States, traveled to Europe on three occasions, and visited Japan. In July 1986, the choir was proud to have been a part of the three-day Liberty Weekend ceremonies surrounding the bicentennial of the Statue of Liberty.

Behind the onstage image of the Boys Choir of Harlem lies the reality of the lives its members lead. Most come from inner-city neighborhoods and schools, environments in which drugs, alcohol, and the many dangers of city streets are part of everyday life. It is not uncommon for a youngster to walk through a neighborhood of abandoned tenements and crack dealers on his way to daily rehearsals. And once he reaches rehearsal, there are often other personal and educational obstacles to overcome. For these youngsters, the choir staff offers individual and family counseling services, as well as tutoring sessions. All of its members graduate from high school, and none experiment with drugs. This is especially gratifying for the staff in light of statistics showing that currently 72 percent of all black children fail to complete high school. The goal of the members is to pursue excellence in whatever they choose to do.

A staff member pointed to a large banner hanging from the ceiling. It reads, "IF YOU CAN'T BE A GREAT TREE, TRY TO BE A GREAT BUSH." It is clear that lives are enhanced, transformed, and indeed saved by the Boys Choir of Harlem program.

Only a small sample of individuals and groups who "reach out" were discussed in this chapter. But there are thousands more. Even a young person, like you, can help by reaching out to friends, peers, and others who might be candidates for seduction by the "quick fix."

5
DRUGS:
AN OLD
STORY

For thousands of years, people all over the world have been altering their ways of thinking and feeling by using drugs. There are many kinds of users, from the pleasure seeker and the escapist to the hospital patient in pain. There are also many categories of drugs, some used by more people than others. Drugs are assigned to groups or categories according to their actions and effects. In Appendix 2, you will find a chart explaining this. In this chapter, some of these categories will be reviewed. Since marijuana, or pot, is the substance many young people experiment with first, the chapter will begin there.

MARIJUANA

ORIGINS AND HISTORY

The Chinese knew of marijuana as long as five thousand years ago. They called it a "giver of light." The people of ancient

India knew it as the "soother of grief." The Chinese used marijuana to treat people suffering from malaria, tension, constipation, and minor illnesses. Although the drug did not actually cure sick people, it made life somewhat more comfortable for them. In India, marijuana was used in religious ceremonies. Religious leaders believed that it could "clear the head and stimulate the brain to think."

In Europe, in the early nineteenth century, writers used psychoactive substances including marijuana to stimulate creativity. The French poet Charles Baudelaire took hashish as well as opium for inspiration. His compatriot, novelist Alexandre Dumas, joined him in experiments with hashish. About 1850, marijuana use began to spread throughout Europe, but it was not until much later, in the second half of the twentieth century, that it became popular.

Marijuana has a fairly long history of use in Mexico and Latin America. Diego Rivera, one of the best-known Mexican artists of the twentieth century, used marijuana. The drug was introduced into the United States around 1915 by Mexican laborers. In the 1920s, musicians were among its most enthusiastic users, and many still use it today, both to compose and to perform. But the widespread use of marijuana in this country was confined mostly to lower socio-economic and minority groups until around 1960, when its use among students and other young people began to increase.

Today, although marijuana is still legal in a few countries of Asia, it is illegal in the United States (except Alaska), Europe, and most other places. It is used by the medical profession to treat glaucoma, and it is said to relieve nausea in patients being treated with chemotherapy for cancer. It is very popular with pleasure-seeking people, among whom are several million Americans.

THE PLANT

Marijuana comes from the cannabis plant, which grows wild in most parts of the world, but is cultivated for the drug in some

Eastern countries and Central and South America. The plant's parts serve several purposes. The stem contains a tough fiber that is used to manufacture cloth and hemp rope, so it is sometimes called the hemp plant. Seeds from the plant are used in bird seed mixtures.

There are male and female cannabis plants. Both plants contain the psychoactive substance, but the female produces larger blooms and more of it. After picking, the flowers and seed heads of the plant are allowed to dry. Dried marijuana ranges in color from grayish green to grayish brown and looks like shredded tobacco. The potency of marijuana depends on the variety of the cannabis plant and the quantity of its principal active chemical, called delta-9 tetrahydrocannabinol (THC). In fact, the plant contains over four hundred different chemicals, but the "high" the user gets is caused by THC, a mind-altering chemical. The more THC in marijuana, the stronger the high will be and the longer it will last. The amount of THC in marijuana is not always the same, because the flower, leaves, and leaf stems contain different amounts. Even the weather and soil can affect the amount of THC in the plant.

*H*OW IT IS USED

Marijuana is usually smoked in cigarettes made from the dried plant material. Hashish, a dark green or brown gumlike resin that is squeezed from the plant's flowers, is most often smoked in pipes—many of which cool the smoke by passing it through water. Hash oil, a crude extract, comes from the cannabis plant too. Like marijuana, the strength of hashish is determined by the amount of THC it contains, but it is generally five to eight times stronger than marijuana. It is subject to deterioration with age and may be relatively weak after longer periods of storage. It is important to distinguish between various potencies, because, like beer and distilled liquors, the stronger preparations have a greater potential for being abused than do the weaker forms of the drug.

A marijuana plant.

INCREASES IN POTENCY OF MARIJUANA

Since 1976, according to law enforcement officials, the American marijuana industry has succeeded in producing a more potent product. In June 1986 health professionals began warning teenagers who use the drug that they are likely to experience extreme highs and suffer their ill effects. Doctors say that this more potent form of marijuana disrupts the user's memory. Studies done for the National Institute on Drug Abuse (NIDA) in 1986 show a rise in the psychoactive agent present in marijuana. For example, the concentration of THC rose from an average of 0.5 percent in 1974 to 1.5 percent in 1986. Dr. Richard Hawks, a member of NIDA's research branch, reported a type of marijuana called sinsemilla, which is cultivated to have no seeds and an especially high THC content in the flowering tops. These have been found to have THC levels of 6.5 percent. "One drag or deep inhalation will get you very high fast," says Dr. Hawks.

MARIJUANA SHORTAGE

The nation's increased efforts to shut down smuggling, combined with a shift of drug dealers into the more profitable cocaine trade, has resulted in a marijuana shortage. As a result, the price has jumped by 50 percent or more in many cities over the last year. In 1987, in Hartford, Connecticut, a narcotics counselor reported prices reaching $1,000 a pound. Drug enforcement agencies in New Jersey say two or three marijuana cigarettes now cost $5.00—$2.00 more than they cost in 1985.

To stop production, helicopters and small two-propeller planes are used to detect marijuana gardens, and then ground teams move in and destroy them. California, New York, Kentucky, Hawaii, and North Carolina are among the states where supplies have been disrupted in this way. Production has also been affected by the cocaine epidemic. "If a person has $20,000 to invest in a drug deal, he'd be crazy to invest it in marijuana," says Dean Latimer, executive editor of *High Times*. "He can make a lot more with cocaine and there's a lot less bulk and risk. It's easier to conceal and it's more profitable."

TEENAGE USE

Marijuana has declined in popularity among teenagers over the past twenty years. In the 1960s, marijuana was a commonplace of youth culture, but studies completed at the University of Michigan show that marijuana use by teenagers has declined from 51 percent in 1980 to 42 percent in 1985.

But more than 40 million people are believed to have tried the drug, and the number of regular users is estimated at 22 million, compared with 5 million for cocaine and 500,000 for heroin. The forces of the illegal drug marketplace, as well as the forces of law, have changed the product dramatically. Because of the success of eradication efforts in Mexico, Colombia, and other countries and a major move against smugglers in south Florida, the quantity of marijuana grown in the United States began to rise in 1985. Many growers used small plots and indoor growing rooms. With less space, they were forced to grow less. So they concentrated on developing more powerful strains that could be sold at higher prices. Also in the United States, marijuana farmers produce the potent sinsemilla strain by separating male and female plants to stop pollination from occurring. This produces flowers with extremely high resin and THC content.

As a result, questioning youngsters about the type of marijuana they smoke is becoming a significant part of drug counseling. "Potency is very important now," says Ellen R. Morehouse, executive director of the Student Assistance Program, which conducts counseling programs in thirty-eight schools in Westchester County, New York.

GETTING HIGH

High is the word most often used when describing the feelings caused by marijuana. Shortly after smoking a marijuana cigarette, a person's perceptions change, particularly his or her perception of time and distance. So one shouldn't drive a car or any other vehicle. The user's coordination and balance are affected. Some people feel silly and laugh about things that wouldn't normally amuse them. Others talk a lot or become quiet. Still others have mild visual or auditory hallucinations. This means that they "see" and "hear" things that may not exist, for example, changes in colors and music. In this high, or "stoned," condition, the smoker experiences a pleasurable calmness or serenity. This is the usual reaction to a small amount of smoking, although some kids become frightened and overly anxious. After a couple of hours, the effects wear off and the smoker's perceptions return to normal.

Although this acute phase only lasts a few hours, some people believe that measurable damage to the user's mental and physical ability can persist much longer. There is evidence that marijuana can remain in the user's system long after it is actually smoked. Traces of the drug have been found in the urine of people who smoked a "joint" a month earlier. For some people, such findings have led to probation, suspension, or dismissal from their jobs, and drug-testing has become a controversial issue. Policemen and other law enforcement officers, in particular, have been affected.

DOES IT REALLY HURT KIDS?

The answer is "Yes." Marijuana affects young people in several ways. First, it interferes with the normal process of growing up, by helping young people avoid facing their problems in a mature way. Using the drug delays developing the ability to assume responsibility for one's behavior.

Secondly, studies show that regular users become psychologically (but not physically) dependent on marijuana. Increasing numbers of kids report having trouble reducing or stopping their marijuana habit.

The physical effects include damage to the lungs when the user inhales the hot unfiltered irritants. The smoke contains some of the cancer-causing agents found in cigarettes. In pregnant females, damage occurs in the reproductive system, which affects the growing fetus. In males, the sperm count is lowered and abnormal sperm cells are found. Since THC is a fat-soluble drug, it is stored in the fatty tissues of the body for a week or more before it is eliminated.

There are emotional problems too. Clinicians report thousands of cases of people with "panic reactions" admitted to hospital emergency rooms after smoking marijuana. Most recover with simple reassurance. But the drug can trigger symptoms of underlying emotional problems and severe psychological disorders like schizophrenia. Smoking marijuana to relieve depression often makes the depression worse. Some doctors have observed an "amotivational syndrome" in young people who smoke pot. The symptoms include apathy, indifference, and a reduction of interests.

Many people believe that the use of marijuana can lead to experimentation with other and often stronger drugs. This is not wholly true, but if someone believes that using one drug helps to escape from problems, it is easy to try another chemical "solution."

One of the consistent effects of regular marijuana use is a decline in school performance. Learning becomes more difficult, memory becomes poor, and thinking is cloudy. Since response and reaction times are also slowed, it is extremely important that a person avoid marijuana if he or she is driving. This is especially true when marijuana and alcohol are taken together, because the combined effects are greater than the effect of one drug taken alone.

CURRENT STATUS

Over the centuries, marijuana has been used in many ways: as a food, a medicine, a religious practice, a symbol, and, simply, a drug. The question of its effects on the brain and the lasting changes in physical and emotional behavior it may cause remain controversial.

While public opinion polls show declining support for the legalization of marijuana, the drug's supporters continue to point out that there is a lack of conclusive evidence that marijuana is more harmful than tobacco or alcohol.

A spokesman for the Washington–based National Organization for the Reform of Marijuana Laws, Jeff Edwards, said the greater potency of marijuana probably means people will smoke less, lowering its potential cancer-causing effects. Scare tactics have not made the drug less attractive to kids.

OPIATES

ORIGINS AND HISTORY

Opiates are often prescribed by doctors to relieve pain. They can be addictive too. Some names may sound familiar, for example, codeine, heroin, and morphine. They all come from a resin taken from the seed of the Asian poppy. The poppy, native to Europe and Asia, has been grown in the Near East since ancient times.

For several thousands of years, people have ingested the milky extract of this plant in order to attain medicinal results and changes in moods. Its chemical name, papaver somniferum, comes from the Latin word *sommus*, the name of the Roman god of sleep. Morphine is an opium by-product and the drug Somnus, which was introduced to the medical world in 1898, is the German name for a morphine by-product.

Opiates are among the oldest drugs used and abused by

human beings. Proof of this has been found in Assyrian poppy art dating from 4000 B.C. and in studies of Egyptian, Greek, and Persian cultures. The poppy plant has been identified in Egyptian tomb paintings and early medical papers. Traces of opiates have even been found in the interiors of funeral perfume jars of the eighteenth through twenty-seventh dynasties of ancient Egyptian rulers. This suggests that narcotics were considered treasures to be preserved for the afterlife.

The ancient Greeks used poppy seeds to relieve pain and produce sleep. In Greek mythology, the poppy was dedicated to Nix, goddess of night; to Thanatos, god of death; to Hypnos, god of sleep; and to Morpheus, god of dreams. The sleep-producing properties of poppy juice were mentioned by the Greek poet Homer as early as 850 B.C., and the use of poppy juice for medical purposes in the form of opium was noted in the writings of the father of medicine, Hippocrates.

The idea that opium was originally Chinese is false. Poppies were grown in Chinese gardens, but only as ornamental flowers and not as a source of opium. Nonetheless, by the nineteenth century, a large number of opiate addicts had developed in China and India. In China, the number of addicts increased at a rapid rate. Attempts to eradicate the profitable narcotic trade lead to the "opium wars" with Great Britain, which China lost.

In Europe, opiates were ordered as tonics for better health. In England, two or three grains dissolved in alcohol was drunk as laudanum for the relief of gastric or stomach pain and neuralgia. (Laudanum is also called tincture of opium). The writers Elizabeth Barrett Browning, Edgar Allan Poe, and Samuel Taylor Coleridge were known to depend upon opiates.

In America, the drug had many users too. A survey of San Francisco at the turn of the century showed that as many as one in every four hundred people abused opiates. Most of them were middle-class American women. Some rubbed the tincture on the bulging gums of infants to ease the pain of teething. However, the extensive social and medical problems of modern opiate addiction began with two additional developments. One was the isolation of purer and stronger opiates such as mor-

A somniferum poppy from which opium is made.

phine; the other was the invention of the hyperdermic needle, which enabled people to inject themselves with the powerful new drugs. Together, these two made possible a rapid euphoria—a more dramatic and pleasurable alteration of mood. The world's first morphine addict was the wife of the man who invented the hyperdermic needle in 1853.

Synthetic Drugs

Around 1880, chemists began experimenting with new compounds based on opium. One of the drugs they produced was heroin, a simple derivative of morphine. Heroin is much stronger than morphine. It is quickly converted into morphine by the body, and small doses have a powerful effect.

Codeine and Demerol are also made from opium compounds. Today, there are hundreds of opiates. Some are semi-synthetic, like heroin, and others are completely synthetic, like Demerol. They all have similar effects but differ in strength, length of action, and in the amount of mood change they produce.

Action of Opiates on the Body

The main effects of opium and its derivatives are on the brain and the bowel. In the brain, the drugs bring relief from pain, suppression of the cough center, stimulation of the vomiting center, relaxation and drowsiness. Some people become anxious, restless, and energetic after taking opiates. Others fall into a sort of light sleep and have vivid dreams.

These drugs cause the pupils of the eyes to contract, sometimes to tiny pin-points. They cause sweating, which can be profuse and uncomfortable. Large doses often produce nausca, vomiting, and depression of breathing. High doses, especially by injection, can cause death by stopping breathing completely.

Opiates are the drugs used most often to treat severe pain. They are also used to control bad coughs. In proper doses, and when needed, opiates are safe and effective. They can paralyze intestinal muscles, so doctors prescribe them for the relief of diarrhea.

DEPENDENCE AND TOLERANCE

The body quickly develops a tolerance for opiates. For example, the usual pain-relieving dose of tincture of opium is twenty drops in a glass of water repeated every four to six hours. In the early part of the nineteenth century in England, a number of writers and artists were addicted to the tincture. The poet Samuel Taylor Coleridge consumed as much as two quarts of tincture every week. The poem "Kubla Khan" was a transcription of one of his opium dreams. Thomas De Quincey, author of *Confessions of an English Opium Eater*, drank up to eight thousand drops a day—the equivalent of one and one-half pints, which would kill a nontolerant person. Although they were dependent on the drug, their bodies had developed a tolerance for large doses.

Different types of drugs create different types of tolerance. For example, the body quickly develops a tolerance for small, "active" doses of sedative drugs, such as alcohol, Seconal, and Valium, but it takes much longer to develop a tolerance for large, potentially lethal doses. This makes users vulnerable to overdoses, because their bodies are unable to cope with large quantities of the drugs. Opiates such as heroin are, in a sense, "safer," because the addict's body is able to develop a tolerance for large doses. Heroin addicts do at times die from overdoses, but such deaths are often associated with the poor quality of drugs bought and sold on the street.

Another significant difference between opiates and other drug categories is the physical result of long-term use. The addict can take opium daily over many years and remain healthy, as long as he or she maintains good hygiene and nutrition practices. Thomas De Quincey is a good example. He started taking the tincture for a toothache in college and died at seventy-four, still an addict.

Withdrawal symptoms begin in an opiate-dependent person four to six hours after the last dose of the drug. Symptoms include diarrhea, abdominal cramps, chills, nausea, sweating, running nose, and tearing eyes. The intensity of these symptoms depends on how much of an opiate was taken, how frequently the user takes the drug, and how long he or she has been using it. Symptoms subside within seven to ten days, although sleeplessness and drug craving can last for months.

TREATMENT

The traditional basic treatment for the opiate addict includes detoxification under supervision in a hospital or as an outpatient, and rehabilitation in various types of therapeutic communities. One controversial form of treatment is "methadone maintenance," in which methadone, a synthetic opiate, is given to the patient as a substitute for the heroin to which he or she has been addicted.

Methadone is taken orally and under supervision. It does not produce euphoria, and there is less depression of the respiratory system than with heroin. The major benefit of substituting one addictive substance for another is a social one. Methadone patients may lead normal lives, rather than turn to crime to support a habit that may cost several hundreds of dollars a day. However, the debate over substituting a new opiate for an old one continues. Counseling, vocational and personal, accompanied by job training helps patients reach the goal of a normal drug-free life.

HALLUCINOGENS AND PCP

More than 600,000 plant species have been categorized. About one in ten thousand of these qualifies as a hallucinogen plant.

Chemicals in these plants act on the central nervous system to produce a state in which the user experiences an alteration of time, consciousness of self, space, and his or her perception of the physical world.

MIND BOGGLING

Here are some quotations from former abusers now in treatment: A fifteen-year-old girl recalls, "I became a butterfly and floated right through closed windows to a bush outside my bedroom window." Another teenager told of fighting off five-inch black and red spiders that covered his entire body. The spiders went through his clothes, leaving circular blue welts as they sucked his blood. His room was filled with the odor of rotten eggs. Yet three hours later, his skin was intact with no visible marks. But he "felt" the pain for two days. A woman six months pregnant reported hearing her baby singing accompanied by organ music. As she stroked her swollen abdomen, the infant responded with gentle kicks. In some clients, senses were interchanged. The smell of garlic became green and the sound of a trumpet was seen as red.

Little is known about the way hallucinogens act in the body. Some psychiatrists have found them to be beneficial in treating patients, but others warn of their dangers and the possibility of inducing insanity and suicide. Physicians usually refer to the drugs as hallucinogens because they cause hallucinations. But this suggests mental illness, so others, who have used or researched the drug, prefer the name psychedelics, a word of Greek origin meaning "mind manifesting." This implies that psychedelic drugs can develop the unused potential of the human mind.

POTENTIAL FOR ABUSE

Hallucinogens or psychedelics have the lowest potential for abuse of any psychoactive drugs. They are considered "safe" by the medical profession, because, even in large doses they do not kill by themselves. Some people use them frequently over many years without physical harm or dependence. Under scientifically approved conditions, they can cause dramatic cures in physical and mental illnesses. The main risk of hallucinogen use is that of a "bad trip," which can result in dangerous behavior or severe depression.

Most hallucinogenic plants taste bitter and cause nausea, vomiting, or other unpleasant physical symptoms soon after they are swallowed. Unusual states of consciousness and fantastic visions seen with closed eyes follow. However, the kind of visions or sensory changes that occur depend upon the circumstances in which hallucinogens are used.

1. INDOLE RING DRUGS

To simplify this review, the drugs are divided into two groups. The first group contains a molecular structure known as the indole ring and is related to hormones made in the brain by the pineal gland. Drugs in this group are LSD (lysergic acid diethylamide), "magic mushrooms" (psilocybin), DMT (dimethyltryptamine) and Yage (ayahuasca caapi).

LSD (Lysergic Acid Diethylamide)

This first group begins with LSD. This drug is synthesized from ergot, a fungus that grows on rye and other grains. Ergot has been around since the Middle Ages. Down through the years, plagues, famine, and mysticism have been associated with the drug. In the eighteenth century, midwives learned how to use the ergot in their practices. They discovered that five to nine of the ergot grains could be given to hasten difficult births without causing hemorrhage afterward. Later, ergot was combined with caffeine to contract dilated blood vessels during migraine headaches.

In 1938, Albert Hofmann, a Swiss chemist working for Sandoz Laboratories, synthesized LSD. Several years later, Hofmann recorded his reactions after taking one quarter of a milligram—a large dose. He experienced six hours of spectacular and dramatic visionary images. Controversy has surrounded the use of the drug ever since. Psychiatrists engaged in research say the effects of the drug are unpredictable. During the 1960s and 1970s, extensive testing programs were secretly carried out by the CIA and the Pentagon in cooperation with the United States Army. In fact, these agencies gave soldiers LSD without their knowledge. (Recently, the Supreme Court ruled that soldiers adversely affected could not sue.) During this period, the drug remained illegal, and the penalties for conviction were harsh.

LSD is one of the most potent drugs known. Although some young users in the 1960s reported feelings of love, union with God, and a deeper understanding of themselves after taking the drug, others had "bad trips." They experienced panic, anxiety attacks, and a fear of losing their minds. Twelve hours later when the drug effects wore off, they remained depressed and anxious for extended periods.

By the 1970s, bad trips were becoming rarer because people had learned how to use the drug intelligently. They took responsible doses in safe settings like their homes and with friends who knew what to expect.

Now LSD comes in many forms, from small, colored tablets and tiny transparent gelatin chips (called "windowpanes") to pieces of paper soaked in solutions of the drug or stamped with ink designs containing it. Occasionally it can be found in capsules or in liquid form. It is usually taken by mouth, but sometimes it is injected.

Despite controversy and bad publicity about the medical dangers of LSD in the 1970s, there is no evidence that it damages chromosomes, injures the brain, or causes any other physical harm, other than in pregnant women.

"Magic Mushrooms" (Psilocybin)

In southern Mexico, mushrooms are important natural psychedelics. They are used in sacred ceremonies and carefully guarded from the outside world. However, in the 1950s, botanists were able to identify the "magic mushrooms" and chem-

A psilocybe mushroom.

ists discovered that their psychoactive properties came from psilocybin, a hallucinogen similar to LSD but whose effects do not last as long.

For a decade, it was believed that the mushrooms could only be found in southern Mexico. But in the 1970s, the mushrooms were found in great numbers in Southeast Asia, in Central and South America, along the Gulf coast of the United States, and in many south-western states. One species grows wild in cow pastures in warm climates. But the psilocybin mushroom can also be cultivated. In fact, kits containing the spores are available in stores and through the mail. Since the spores don't contain psilocybin, they are not illegal, allowing thousands of people the chance to produce and distribute magic mushrooms.

Potency varies in wild and cultivated mushrooms. Dried or lightly cooked mushrooms taste bitter and are less likely to cause discomfort. Because they are easy to eat and their effects are short-lived, they are an attractive psychedelic. In addition, there are no aftereffects like the sluggishness experienced with LSD.

DMT (dimethyltryptamine)

DMT is a simple chemical that resembles certain hormones made in the brain. The compound is easily made in laboratories. In the 1960s, synthetic DMT was sold on the black market.

DMT is one psychedelic that cannot be taken by mouth. Users smoke it or inject it, and South American Indians use DMT plants prepared as powdered snuffs. This snuff is called "yopo," and the men blow it forcefully through long tubes into each others' nose. This is extremely painful. Intoxication follows immediately and is very intense, although it lasts only thirty minutes or less. While under its influence, the Indians dance, sing, and see visions of god and spirits.

Yage (Ayahuasca Caapi)

Yage (pronounced yah-hay) is a strong psychedelic drink made from a woolly vine of the Amazon forests. Indians pound pieces of the vine with stones and then cook the greens in water. This brew is used in all-night vision-seeking rituals at coming-of-age ceremonies for adolescent boys. Indians believe the spirit of the vine enters their bodies and enables them to have visions of jungles and jungle animals, especially jaguars. Many think the drug helps them see into the future and communicate telepathically over long distances. Physically, yage causes intense vomiting and diarrhea, followed by a state more relaxed and dreamy than that resulting from LSD use. This euphoria lasts from six to ten hours.

2. HALLUCINOGENS RELATED TO ADRENALINE AND AMPHETAMINES

The second group of hallucinogens resemble molecules of adrenaline or amphetamines. These drugs may make people feel high very quickly, but a peak may not be reached for several hours. Some users find them less dramatic than LSD and its relatives, although in large doses the adrenaline relatives are more toxic than the indoles in the first group. Peyote and mescaline, STP (Dom), and a variety of synthetic drugs are in the group. Peyote is the oldest drug known to native Americans, so the review begins with that drug.

Peyote

Peyote is a corruption of the word *peyott,* which means "silk cacoon." Many accounts have been written about various aspects of peyote as it is used in Mexico, and this has added to the mystery of the plant.

Many ceremonies have developed around the use of peyote. A typical example involves a burning open fire where groups partake of the sacred plant. The Indians chant and sing. During the ritual as many as sixty-four "buttons" may be eaten, although the usual number is from four to twelve. The buttons are formed by slicing and drying the above-ground portion of the plant. The fibrous slices will dissolve in the mouth, except for the fibers, which are swallowed whole. Participants in the ceremony are shown the "way" on the road to the good life. The Indians enjoy oneness with their fellow men and with nature. They are transported to a new world of sensibility and intelligence. For the Indians, peyote use is essentially religious, as opposed to the pleasure-seeking experience of most European or nonnative Americans.

Mescaline

Mescaline was isolated from peyote in 1894. It is the only naturally occurring psychedelic in this family of adrenaline-related drugs. Throughout the twentieth century, a few professionals and artists have experimented with it. Aldous Huxley, the British writer, philosopher, and author of *Brave New World*, experimented extensively with mescaline in the 1950s. But there was no general demand for it until the psychedelic revolution of the 1960s. Then black market mescaline began to appear.

Since the drug sells for a higher price than LSD, many unscrupulous dealers sold LSD as mescaline. Real mescaline comes as long, needlelike white crystals. Half a gram is the usual dose. The pure drug may cause initial nausea, though not as frequently as peyote. Its effects last up to twelve hours and generally resemble those of peyote.

Mescaline can be synthesized in the laboratory, but it is called a natural drug, because the molecules already exist in nature. Although it is not as strong as LSD, its effects are similar. Mescaline is usually smoked or swallowed in the form of capsules or tablets.

STP (Dom)

STP is a synthetic drug that resembles mescaline in its chemical structure. In the 1960s, overdoses caused by black market tablets gave STP a bad reputation. It has few users now.

MDA (Methylemedioxyamphetamine) and Related Drugs

In the drug subculture, MDA is known as the "love drug," because it is supposed to generate loving feelings in group participants. It is a strong stimulant and chemically related to amphetamines. Some users claim it has a calming and relaxing effect. But high doses can cause unpleasant muscular tensions, especially in the facial muscles. MDA combined with alcohol or other depressants can result in adverse reactions. Snorting or injecting the drug is considered extremely dangerous.

Other drugs in this series, like MMDA, PMA, or TMA, are not found on the streets. They are still being developed in pharmacological laboratories.

*H*ALLUCINOGENS: BAD AND GOOD

"Bad trips" are the greatest danger of these drugs. Since users must depend upon black market dealers, drugs are not always first-class or pure. Users cannot be certain of dosage or potency and frequently suffer ill effects.

Psychedelics act as intensifiers. This means that if you take them when you are despondent or depressed, they make you feel more unhappy. Since they are stimulants, the user has abnormal feelings that can interfere with daily routines like school or work.

*P*CP (ANGEL DUST)

PCP (phencyclidine) doesn't come from a plant but from a laboratory. This is a strange drug that doesn't quite fit any category. It can be an anesthetic, but it is not a depressant. It is not really a psychedelic either, but is usually thought of as part of that group. It was made in a pharmaceutical laboratory in the late 1950s and introduced to United States medical practitioners in 1963 under the trade name of Sernyl. It was used as a surgical anesthetic, but proved to be less effective than the traditional ether. Patients reported unpleasant side effects, including hallucination. In 1965, the drug was withdrawn from the market for human use. Two years later, it reappeared as a veterinary anesthetic. Animals could not report their reactions to the drug, so no one really knows how it affected them.

PCP is a cheap and easy drug to make. It comes in a pure white crystallike powder or a tablet or capsule. Users swallow, smoke, inject, or sniff the drug. The powdered angel dust can be sprinkled on marijuana cigarettes, or herbs like parsley, oregano, and mint. Some people dissolve the powder in an organic solvent and spray it on "joints," which are then called "dusters."

The physical effects depend on the size of the dose, how it is used, and the condition of the user. Users report increased heart rate, breathing and pulse rate, flushing, sweating, decreased sensation to pain, and impaired coordination. Large doses can lead to convulsion and death.

The mental effects vary but often include apathy, distortion of time and space perception, and disorganized thinking. Regular use affects memory, concentration, and judgment.

In recent years, PCP has become a popular drug among young people living in decaying urban areas. This caused people to associate PCP with crime and violence. However, there is no evidence that PCP automatically makes users become violent or commit crimes. Young people don't automatically become criminals because they take drugs.

One big problem with PCP is that it can be sold to unsuspecting buyers as other, more desirable drugs. Pills have been sold as synthetic THC, the psychoactive ingredient in marijuana. Neighborhood vegetable-stand variety mushrooms, treated with PCP alone or with PCP and LSD, were sold as magic mushrooms in the 1970s. PCP-LSD combinations have been sold as mescaline in the black market to naive thrill seekers.

PCP can produce bizarre behavior in people who are normally quite calm and reserved. Under the influence of the drug, accidental drownings, falls, and automobile fatalities may occur. A mental disturbance or a disturbance of the user's thought processes (a PCP psychosis) may last for days.

INHALANTS

Most people do not think of inhalants as drugs, because they were not meant to be sold as drugs, and they can be bought so easily. They include solvents, aerosols, some anesthetics, and other chemicals. Many of them can be found in homes. Examples are hair sprays, fingernail polish remover, lighter and cleansing fluids, paint sprays, and some glues. Anesthetics include nitrous oxide (laughing gas) and halthan. Among commonly abused inhalants are amyl nitrite and butyl nitrite.

The fumes of some organic solvents have strong chemical odors and make people feel lightheaded, hot, and dizzy. Young people often experiment with them as their introduction to drugs.

ORGANIC SOLVENTS

Model airplane glue, rubber cement, gasoline and cleaning fluid, paint thinner, varnish, and some waxes contain organic solvents. When sniffed, they act as psychoactive drugs and cause dizziness and nausea. In large doses, they may induce visual hallucinations and impairment of judgment. The effects are almost immediate, since inhaling puts the chemical into the bloodstream and brain very fast. Children who sniff regularly develop a tolerance to organic solvents and a habit that is difficult to break. They are unable to perform in school and are apathetic and detached from the world around them.

Glue became the most popular solvent inhalant among children over the years, and continues to be so today. The users, in the past, have been between ten and seventeen years old and were mostly Hispanic and Native American males. However, easy availability and the power to dramatically change consciousness very fast make inhaling solvents attractive to many other young people.

AEROSOL SPRAYS

Until the early 1980s, most pressurized cans contained a type of fluorocarbon known by its brand name: Freon. When inhaled, Freon produced the same psychological effects as organic solvents. Chemists and environmental activists became increasingly alarmed about the amount of Freon being sprayed into the air and possible damage to the earth's atmosphere. Some manufacturers switched to other propellants, but these also cause change in consciousness when people inhale them.

Because the cans have several chemicals in them, some people spray the can's contents into a bag or balloon so that the particles separate from the Freon gas by sticking to the sides of the bag. They then sniff from the bag. Others inhale the sprays through a cloth filter.

AMYL NITRITE (AMYS, SNAPPERS, POPPERS, PEARLS)

Amyl nitrite is an inhalant—a breathable chemical with mind-altering vapors. It is a clear yellowish liquid with a strong smell. It is packaged in inhalers and in cloth-covered, sealed glass capsules. When the capsule is broken, it makes a popping or snapping sound, hence the nicknames "snappers" and "poppers."

This simple chemical has been used for more than one hundred years to relieve chest pain in people with coronary artery disease. When these patients exert themselves, they suffer severe chest pains. Breathing the fumes of amyl nitrite lessens the pain, because the drug dilates arteries throughout the body, thereby reducing the heart's workload.

Other physical effects may include a throbbing or brief pounding headache, sudden fall in blood pressure, dizziness and nausea, warmth of the skin, and a change in consciousness that resembles fainting.

Before 1960, amyl nitrite was a prescription drug. Most

users who carried it with them for use in emergencies did not consider it a mind-altering substance. However, some people did use it recreationally, especially after the Food and Drug Administration removed the prescription requirement.

But during the 1960s, users of street drugs experimented with amyl nitrite as a cheap, quick, and legal way to get high. Among young people who liked to sniff organic solvents like glue, the drug had special appeal.

Amyl nitrite gained a reputation for enhancing sexual experience among male homosexuals. The drug was supposed to intensify and prolong orgasm. As recreational use spread, authorities became alarmed, and in 1969, the Food and Drug Administration reimposed the prescription requirement.

All nitrites are considered poisonous in excess, but when amyl nitrite is inhaled, it breaks down easily and leaves the body very quickly. It is considered one of the safest drugs in medicine, and even frequent use doesn't appear to bother people. Nonetheless, long-term use may have harmful effects that have yet to be identified.

People with anemia, hypertension, glaucoma, and recent head injuries should never use amyl nitrite. The drug causes a sudden drop in blood pressure (hypotension), which can produce loss of coordination, fainting, flushed face and neck, dizziness, and headache.

BUTYL NITRITE AND ISOBUTYL NITRITE (LOCKER ROOM, RUSH)

These are close chemical relatives of amyl nitrite and are not under any drug regulation. They can be obtained through the mail or over-the-counter in head shops. They are known as "locker room" and "rush," because they can produce a high that lasts from a few seconds to several minutes. Physical effects take place immediately and are similar to those caused by "poppers."

STIMULANTS

Stimulants are drugs that make people feel energetic and wide-awake and give them the desire to increase physical activity. Some drugs are found in plants, others are made in the laboratory, but they all raise the energy level of the nervous system in similar ways.

HOW THE BODY REACTS TO THEM

Stimulant drugs work by causing nerve fibers to release the chemical noradrenaline, which is related to the hormone adrenaline and is also a stimulant neurotransmitter. The stimulation people feel when they take these drugs is really a result of the body's own chemical energy going to work in the nervous system. The drugs just make the body expend it sooner and in greater quantity than it would ordinarily.

This release of chemical energy causes changes in the mind and body. A person feels happy, alert, eager, and excited. There is an increase in heart rate and blood pressure.

WHY PEOPLE TAKE THEM

Any high school or college student knows the sense of panic one feels the night before a final examination or a due date for a term report. Stimulants are popular because they give temporary control over rhythms of wakefulness and force the brain to concentrate instead of going to sleep. The nervous system releases some of its reserved chemical energy to keep a person awake and alert, so that he or she can complete the required studying.

Athletes believe they perform better on stimulants, because the nerves and muscles receive more attention with the use of these drugs. Driving long distances after using a stimulant may provide a sense of confidence and safety, since the driver feels wide awake and alert.

Stimulants suppress hunger and are very popular with females, especially those who are trying to lose weight. For some people, these drugs can change a moderate depression to a lighter mood.

DANGERS OF STIMULANTS

After the stimulant wears off, the body is left with less energy than usual and must replenish its supplies. People experience a letdown that may make them lethargic, sleepy, lazy, or even depressed.

Most people are impatient and don't want to give the body time to re-adjust. They just want to experience that feeling again, so they take another dose of the drug. Repeated use of stimulants produces dependence, and soon any excuse is a good one for using the drug. The most popular stimulant in America is coffee. It has been said that our whole economy is built around the coffee break.

COFFEE AND CAFFEINE

Avicenna, the famous tenth-century Arabian philosopher and physician, was one of the first people to write about coffee. Because of its association with the Arab world, Linnaeus, a Swedish botanist of the eighteenth century, named the plant coffea arabica. The original home of this plant was Ethiopia.

In 1601, coffee was introduced into England, where William Parry gave it its contemporary spelling. The beverage was so popular that it soon spread across Europe. And by 1689, coffee had reached the United States with the opening of a café in Boston, Massachusetts. Demand for the drink eventually became so great that world powers began to grow the plants in their colonies.

In the eighteenth century, South America became the center of coffee's cultivation. Now two-thirds of the world's supply of coffee comes from Brazil, packed in 132-pound bags.

It takes 40 million of these bags, or over 5 billion pounds, to supply the world's annual requirements.

Famous people like Johann Sebastian Bach and Honoré de Balzac were coffee addicts. Dependence is very common in the West to this day. Many people claim that they can't concentrate or get going in the morning without having a cup of coffee first.

It is not unusual for some people to have four cups a day, even though coffee is irritating to the lining of the stomach. To compensate, these people constantly take antacids. Heavy and frequent drinkers never give the body time or a chance to replenish its stores of chemical energy and come to rely more and more on coffee.

When a person drinks two cups of coffee, the effects begin in 15 to 30 minutes. The person's metabolism, body temperature, and blood pressure may increase. Other effects include increased urine production, higher blood sugar levels, hand tremors, delayed sleep, loss of coordination, and decreased appetite. Large doses may cause nausea, trembling, and headache.

Coffee and caffeine have been linked to birth defects. The evidence is inconclusive, but pregnant women are warned not to consume coffee or tea. Recent medical findings have established a possible connection between coffee and cancer of the pancreas. Drinking coffee in moderation appears to be the wisest practice.

COLAS

Cola is a caffeine-containing seed from the cola tree. Popular bottled cola drinks like Coca Cola, Pepsi Cola, and Tab have little cola nut in them, but may contain synthetic caffeine. The controversy regarding caffeine in soft drinks has caused many firms to produce colas without caffeine. But one must read the list of contents to be sure. Some people drink soft drinks to an excess believing they are quenching their thirst. But sugar and caffeine are habit forming and high in calories, giving them the potential for abuse.

COCOA AND CHOCOLATE

Another source of caffeine is chocolate, which comes from the tropical cacoa tree (pronounced *cah-cow*). Its seeds are cacoa or cocoa beans. The fat in these seeds is cocoa butter. White chocolate is the butter mixed with sugar. The roasted, ground beans, with the fat removed, become cocoa. Regular chocolate is made by adding extra fat to roasted ground beans.

"Chocoholics" or "chocolate freaks" consume an excess of chocolate, particularly during binges. Many of these abusers are not aware of their involvement with the drug caffeine, although their consumption patterns are similar to those addicted to coffee, tea, or cola drinks.

COCAINE

Cocaine is a drug extracted from the leaves of the coca plant, which grows in the hot, humid valley of the coastal slopes of the Andes. It has been cultivated by the Indians of South America for thousands of years. In Peru and Bolivia, the leaves of the plant are chewed by large numbers of people as a stimulant and as a medicine.

Coca contains fourteen drugs, of which cocaine is the most important. The vitamins and minerals in the plants' leaves are important supplements to the Indians' diets. The Indians make a wad of dry leaves rubbed with powdered lime and then chew and suck this wad for thirty minutes, swallowing the juices. Chewing makes the mouth and tongue numb, but the effects come quickly. Unlike coffee, coca soothes the stomach and doesn't cause the user to become jittery. It is more powerful than caffeine and produces a good mood.

TONIC AND ANESTHETIC

About 1880, Coca-Cola became popular as a tonic or soft drink. At that time, it contained coca, which had a stimulating effect.

Meanwhile scientists isolated the drug cocaine from the plants' leaves and made it available to doctors in the form of a pure white powder. Because it was the first local anesthetic, cocaine was a blessing to surgeons who performed operations with minor painkillers. In their eagerness to help humanity, doctors began to prescribe cocaine for almost everything—including addiction to alcohol and opiates.

By 1910, the medical profession realized that cocaine had addictive powers too, and doctors discontinued its widespread use for patients. The Coca-Cola Company took cocaine out of its tonic. Subsequently, safer anesthetics were developed, and now doctors use cocaine only for certain eye, nose, and throat operations.

COCAINE ABUSE

Besides the white, crystallike powder frequently seen, cocaine comes in large pieces, which are called "rocks" on the street. Another form, smoked in South America, is paste.

When cocaine is smoked or sniffed, the intense effects begin within a few minutes, peak within 15 to 20 minutes, and disappear within an hour. These effects include dilated pupils and an increase in heart rate, blood pressure, temperature, and respiration.

Some people prefer to shoot or inject cocaine intravenously, which gives an even faster and more intense reaction. Smoking crack, a specially prepared form of cocaine, puts cocaine into the bloodstream even faster than an intravenous injection. After the "rush," a brief period of euphoria, the user may feel tired, unhappy, and lethargic. Eager to return to that feeling of euphoria, the user smokes again as soon as possible.

Among the South American Indians, there is little abuse of cocaine. However, in the United States, using cocaine is fashionable and very expensive. The drug costs up to $3,000 an ounce in some cities. Crack may cost even more for the dealer or supplier, although it reaches the street as a cheap item. Occasional use in social settings is apparently not harmful. But as the users' stories in Chapter 3 show, cocaine and crack are addictive, dangerous, and sometimes deadly.

People who use large doses for extended periods may become paranoid with auditory, visual, and tactile hallucinations. Preparing the drug for freebasing is in itself dangerous. Accidents occurring when people use volatile solvents have caused serious burns and death. The comic Richard Pryor suffered serious burns when freebasing several years ago.

People who use cocaine repeatedly because they like its effects can reach the point of centering their lives around getting and using the drug. The recent mounting popularity of crack is associated with crime, violence, and youth in America today.

AMPHETAMINES

These drugs have chemical names, but they're better known by their street names, such as "speed," "uppers," "drexies" or "bennies." Their real names are amphetamine, dextroamphetamine, and methamphetamine. They are synthetic and were first manufactured in Germany in the 1930s. The drugs' chemical structures are similar to those of adrenaline, the body's own stimulant. Amphetamines are more toxic than cocaine and, when abused, can cause worse problems.

During the 1950s and 1960s, the pharmaceutical industry manufactured large quantities of amphetamines, which somehow found their way to the black market. Doctors were urged by the industry to prescribe them for depressed housewives and people with weight problems.

The drug raises the body's blood pressure and breathing rates but decreases the appetite. In addition, the user may have a dry mouth, headache, and blurred vision and may sweat and become anxious.

Frequent use of large amounts of amphetamines can cause brain damage. As with heroin and other drugs used intravenously, people who inject themselves with dirty needles and contaminated drugs can get serious infections in the heart and lungs and suffer strokes or kidney damage.

Some people experience a psychological dependence on amphetamines. These users continue to use the drug to avoid the "down" mood they get when the drug's effect wears off.

LOOK-ALIKES ARE RISKY

"Look-alikes" are pills and capsules that are made to look like amphetamines but contain no controlled substances. They can be bought across the counter, by mail order, or on the street. They may contain caffeine or ephedrine or both. Phenylpropanolamine is a synthetic drug that is added to many cold remedies and some over-the-counter diet pills.

Some states have laws that prohibit look-alikes, so new drugs called "act-alikes" have appeared. The drugs don't physically resemble prescription or over-the-counter drugs. These act-alikes, called "speed" and "uppers," can be bought on the street and are expensive, even though they are not as strong as amphetamines.

Because these drugs are easily available, young people tend to find them attractive. Once they begin using them, they may be at high risk for using other and more powerful drugs.

SEDATIVE-HYPNOTICS

Sedative-hypnotics are drugs that act as depressants. These drugs slow down the body's functions. This large category includes "sleeping pills," alcohol, and certain tranquilizers. They are "sedative" because they calm anxiety, and "hypnotic" because they promote sleep.

ALCOHOL

Alcohol is one of the world's oldest and most popular drugs. Down through the ages, people have used alcohol to change their moods and behavior. Ethyl alcohol, or alcohol, is called a social and recreational drug, because people use it to make them relax, lose that "up-tight" feeling, become friendly, and more confident.

Many people think of alcohol as being a stimulant, because it is used to initiate activity, get one in a party mood, or increase productivity. But this is false and misleading. Alcohol is a depressant. It depresses the nervous system. One or two drinks may make some people lively, alert, and talkative, but three or four can make them drunk and impair brain function.

Production of ethyl alcohol depends upon yeast, which feeds on sugar, making alcohol and carbon dioxide as by-products. The chemical formula for the colorless, inflammable, and powerful drug is C_2H_5OH.

Wine and beer were the earliest sources of alcohol. Wine pressed from grapes is one of the oldest products made for human consumption. Records of the grape, its cultivation, and its wine are found in the Old Testament of the Bible: "And Noah began to be a husbandman [farmer] and he planted a vineyard. And he drank the wine and was drunken."

Brewing beer from fermented grain is as old a practice as making wine from fermented grapes. Brewing was known to be in practice as early as 5000 B.C. in Egypt.

The skilled brewers of the Middle Ages were mostly monks in monasteries, but in the sixteenth and seventeenth centuries, more and more commercial breweries were built. Beer became so popular that in 1634, Charles I imposed the first excise tax on ale and beer.

Today, beer is one of America's favorite drinks. In 1984, the United States Brewers Association reported that annual consumption had reached 182,474 million barrels, an average of 24 gallons per person.

Whiskey and other hard liquors are the strongest of the

three kinds of alcoholic beverages used the most. Unlike beer and wine, they are made by a distillation process. Brandy was the first distilled liquor ever made. It was the result of heating wine and then cooling and condensing the vapors in another container. Many more distilled liquors are manufactured now. Scotch and bourbon whiskey are made from beerlike preparations of grain. Rum is distilled from fermented molasses; gin and vodka are diluted ethyl alcohol (but gin has flavor added) and are also distilled from grain. Because of their high alcohol content, these hard liquors are stronger and more intoxicating than fermented drinks such as wine and beer.

Alcohol is absorbed very quickly. It is not digested like food, but enters the bloodstream and travels through the body. When it reaches the brain, it affects centers that control speech, vision, and coordination.

The job of breaking down chemicals in a drug (called oxidation) is done mainly by the liver. Because alcohol is a toxic chemical, regular use over many years can cause serious physical damage. Cirrhosis of the liver, in which normal cells are replaced by useless fibrous tissue, is a common illness. The brain and nervous, digestive, respiratory, and circulatory systems are also damaged by the poisonous effects of alcohol.

Blackouts, which are losses of memory during periods of heavy drinking, can occur. Hallucinations, such as hearing voices and seeing things, is another frequently occurring syndrome. A heavy drinker's attitude and behavior may change, and friends tend to avoid him or her.

People who cannot control their drinking are called alcoholics. They are sick with the disease alcoholism. About 10 percent of people who drink become alcoholics. In 1987, there were more than 17 million of them in the United States. They belong to every racial group and live in all kinds of neighborhoods. Most are married, employed, and have families.

There is no single cause of alcoholism. Most professionals believe that a combination of physical, mental, and emotional factors may be involved. Some scientists believe alcoholism may be inherited, because children of alcoholics tend to become alcoholics in large numbers, although many people whose parents never drank at all also become alcoholics. Other researchers are looking at physical causes like allergies, vitamin deficiency, or even enzyme imbalance as clues to the cause of alcoholism.

There is no one treatment plan that works successfully for everyone. But statistics show that 80 percent of all alcoholics *can* be rehabilitated. Medical professionals, social workers, psychologists, and counselors working alone or in combination usually provide treatment. Alcoholics Anonymous (AA) is a vital part of treatment. But the drinker must want to change his or her behavior. No one can be forced into successful treatment. Since this is a family disease, special AA groups for spouses and children of alcoholics provide additional information, support, and guidance.

BARBITURATES

These sedative-hypnotic drugs, known as sleeping pills, are manufactured both legally and illegally. Doctors prescribe them in low doses to lessen anxiety, and in higher doses to induce sleep.

Barbituric acid was discovered in 1864. The first barbiturate sleeping drug was called barbital. It appeared in 1903 and was followed by phenobarbital in 1912. There are hundreds of barbiturates in current use. Some are long acting, lasting twelve to twenty-four hours. They don't produce euphoria, so people take them for their sedative effect rather than to get high.

Other, short-acting barbiturates are metabolized rapidly by the liver, and their effects last six to seven hours. These drugs act much like alcohol, causing pleasant feelings in low doses. Some people use them to create a mood change.

There are short-acting barbiturates that produce almost immediate unconsciousness when injected into the veins. Pentathal is a good example. It is used as an anesthetic for surgical operations. Short-acting barbiturates are also called "downers."

Tolerance can develop with either drug group. But tolerance to the effects on mood develops faster than tolerance to the lethal dose. This means as users increase the dose to get the same effect, they can risk death by taking barbiturates regularly. Eventually, the dose they need to fall asleep after drinking could be the dose that stops them breathing.

Alcohol and barbiturates are particularly dangerous when used together, because of the accumulative depressant effect. The combination can be deadly.

Taking downers to help cope with feelings of low self-esteem or depression is a risky way to use the drugs. Like alcohol, the drug may mask the symptoms temporarily, but eventually severely increase the depression.

Some downers are not barbiturates. They have brand names, including Quaalude, Sopor, and Mandrax. Their effects are similar to those caused by barbiturates, but less likely to depress the respiratory center in cases of overdose. Quaalude and wine together produce a euphoric state that is called "luding out" on the street. Quaalude has a street reputation as a sex enhancer and a party drug. Like all downers and like alcohol, the drug can lower inhibition and reduce anxiety.

One of the oldest sleeping drugs is chloral hydrate. In old Westerns and in mystery films, chloral hydrate is the "knockout drops" slipped into unsuspecting young maidens' or potential hijack victims' drinks. Other nonbarbiturate downers are Doriden, Placidyl, and paraldehyde, which are used in medicine as hypnotics.

TRANQUILIZERS

There are major and minor tranquilizers. A major one is Thorazine, which is used to control psychotic patients. Minor tranquilizers are the newer products of the pharmacology industry and include Librium, Valium, and Dalmane. They are very popular, and millions of people take them to relieve anxiety and induce calmness. However, they have the potential to produce adverse effects and dependence.

The minor tranquilizers provide a few advantages over

barbiturates. They are safer in a case of overdose, less dangerous with alcohol, and not as likely to cause a dramatic withdrawal syndrome when long-term use ceases. Used for daytime sedatives, they cause less drowsiness than barbiturates.

Women's groups have criticized doctors for often prescribing minor tranquilizers for depressed or bored housewives, female executives, and worried coeds. Nonetheless, the drugs remain the most prescribed in the world. Customers are cautioned not to use the drugs to solve deep emotional problems that need professional attention and treatment.

EPILOGUE

This book was written not only to help young people learn more about drugs and their actions, but to give hope to those kids and their families who are trying to live drug-free lives, especially those who have substituted drugs in the past for adequate coping skills. To them, there is daylight at the end of the tunnel.

To gather data for this book, more than two hundred kids in the last phase of an eighteen-month residential, drug-free treatment program were asked to identify what factors they thought were influential in their addiction. They replied this way:

Percentage	Responses
67%	Lack of self-confidence
20%	Inferiority complex
13%	Loneliness

The teenage responses are simplistic and not scientifically valid. But they reflect an adolescent tendency to respond emotionally and spontaneously to a complex question. However, fifty professionals, who specialize in substance abuse treatment, were asked a similar question about initial teenage drug use. The professionals' replies were:

Percentage	Responses
62%	Exposure to drugs
20%	Ignorance of the risks of drug use and the nature of the addictive process
18%	Genetic factors

Many professionals believe the environment of a drug-oriented society tends to negate their efforts in education and prevention. These professionals say, "No drugs, no abuse." Others have different opinions. One is Sterling Johnson, special prosecutor for the District Attorney's Office in New York City, who knows that there is no simple solution. "Drug abuse is a complex problem. Harsh laws against drug dealing and selling with stiff jail sentences are not a deterrent. It's not wholly the profit factor either. We have to take a hard look at what makes people want to take drugs. Those answers are still unclear. It has to be education, prevention, treatment, and medical research and law enforcement all working together. This is a drug-oriented society and has been so for many years. Any real change can only come from commitment on the part of many people, especially those in high places like our Congress. The type of committment I mean must come from both sides of the aisle in Congress where we mobilize all of our resources and our best brains in an all-out effort. Somewhat like we did for the moon shot," Johnson says enthusiastically.

Dr. Lorraine Hale is the daughter of Mother Hale, who for years has cared for deserted and abandoned babies of addicted mothers. Many of the babies were left on her door step with notes reading, "Please take care of my baby. I cannot." Dr. Hale, executive director of Hale House, feels that adults need to assume more responsibility in the guidance of young people. "Adults forget the pain, trauma, and problems of being a teenager. I don't believe peer pressure has a great deal of influence on peer behavior. Kids are looking for something to ease that hurt and pain they are experiencing. Kids know drugs are bad for you, but they still experiment, take a chance, because their youth, insecurity, and vulnerability leave them few choices."

Dr. Hale speaks with authority about minority youngsters. "For black children, drugs may be seen as the only out. Not only do they have their own pain and anger, but they have the hostility of their families. It is well documented that too many of these kids live in homes where they get little, if any, love and affection. They are fed and clothed, but that's all."

Hope for the future . . . "Youth Day" in New York City's Bryant Park (a known drug-dealing hot spot) honors Youthful Drug Fighters. "It appears that dealers become nervous when youngsters play there. The dealers stay away," say the police.

Mother Hale cuddling some of her "children." She gives them love and nurturing that gets them started in a new direction.

Similarly, in many cases, Dr. Hale feels that white young-sters are asked to compete, get the best grades, and make the prestigious colleges. "They endure the same trauma." She pauses for a long moment. "No one is ever asked to be what he is or is loved for what he is . . . or accepted for what he is." Dr. Hale reveals that in all of her professional years, she has yet to see a pusher chasing a kid or pushing a needle in one's arm. "Children do this to themselves. Can't people see to what lengths kids go to ease the pain? Professionals are looking in the wrong places. It's important that we look at the child, his family and his environment. And look at what society has taken from children."

For those emerging from a long, black tunnel into brilliant sunshine, we congratulate you for breaking the connection.

*G*ETTING HELP:
THE RIGHT TREATMENT PROGRAM

You may be asked about a treatment program, or you might want to refer a friend or acquaintance to one. How do you know which is a good treatment program? What does a good treatment program offer? Is there one just for adolescents?

Dr. Mark S. Gold, director of research at the Regent Hospital in New York City and medical director of the National Cocaine Helpline, offers some suggestions:

> In general, an outpatient treatment program is far more preferable for someone than hospitalization. But sometimes hospitalization can't be avoided. If you or someone you know is seeking treatment help here are the questions to weigh with a trained professional to determine the mode of treatment:
>
> 1. How severe is the drug abuse problem? Is the drug use so uncontrollable that the user can't stop at all? Is the user taking large amounts of drugs, such as freebasing or using drugs intravenously?

2. Is the person physically addicted to several drugs? If so, will he or she need detoxification? (This is done only in hospitals.)

3. Are severe psychiatric and behavioral problems present as a result of the drug use? Have other medical problems occurred, such as severe weight loss, gastritis, or insomnia? Has the person become suicidal or violent?

4. Is the user's daily function interrupted? Can the user take care of him or herself, go to work, school, or relate to other people?

5. Has the patient failed in other outpatient treatment attempts?

Once these questions are answered and you have a better idea of the severity of a drug problem, a decision as to type of treatment can be made.

Usually, the success rates of any type of program depends on the person as much as the program. The person must be ready to admit that help is needed and he or she is ready to participate in that help. Sometimes, if the drug problem is not severe and the user has strong motivation to be drug-free, then, with family support, the possibility of success is good. People who functioned well before they had trouble with drugs can usually function well after drug use ceases. "If they can make the life-style changes needed and incorporate total abstinence into their lives, there is a high probability of success," concludes Dr. Gold.

Successful programs for youth have been designed especially for that age group. Many are short-term inpatient with continued outpatient care for a year or two. All include psychological, educational, medical, and vocational services tailored to adolescent needs. All include work with families of the client.

APPENDIX 1
WHERE TO GET INFORMATION

ALCOHOLICS ANONYMOUS
(Most towns and cities everywhere—check telephone directory)

BLUE CROSS/BLUE SHIELD OF GREATER NEW YORK
622 Third Avenue
New York, New York 10017

NARCOTICS ANONYMOUS
57 East 11 Street
New York, New York 10003

NATIONAL ASSOCIATION OF CHILDREN OF ALCOHOLICS, INC.
P.O. Box 421691
San Francisco, California 94142

NATIONAL CLEARINGHOUSE FOR ALCOHOL INFORMATION
Department ATF
P.O. Box 2345
Rockville, Maryland 20892

NATIONAL CLEARINGHOUSE FOR DRUG ABUSE INFORMATION
P.O. Box 416
Department DQ
Kensington, Maryland 20795

NATIONAL CONGRESS OF PARENTS AND TEACHERS
700 North Rush Street
Chicago, Illinois 60611-2571

NATIONAL COUNCIL ON ALCOHOLISM
12 West 21 Street, 7th Floor
New York, New York 10010

NATIONAL INSTITUTE ON DRUG ABUSE CLEARINGHOUSE
Parklawn Building, Room 10A-43
5600 Fishers Lane
Rockville, Maryland 20857

NATIONAL SAFETY COUNCIL
444 Michigan Avenue
Chicago, Illinois 60601

OAKLAND PARENTS IN ACTION
Pacific Institute
1401 Franklin Street, Suite 610
Oakland, California 94612

OPERATION CORK
8939 Villa La Jolla Drive
San Diego, California 92037

PACIFIC INSTITUTE FOR RESEARCH AND EVALUATION
JUST SAY NO Materials
7104 Wisconsin Avenue
Bethesda, Maryland 20814

SUPERINTENDENT OF DOCUMENTS
U.S. Government Printing Office
Washington, D.C. 20452

THE AMERICAN COUNCIL FOR DRUG EDUCATION
5820 Hubbard Drive
Rockville, Maryland 20852

THE CHRISTOPHER D. SMITHERS FOUNDATION, INC.
P.O. Box 67
Mill Neck, New York 11765

U.S. DEPARTMENT OF HEALTH AND HUMAN SERVICES
Alcohol, Drug Abuse, and Mental Health Administration
Rockville, Maryland 20857

WISCONSIN CLEARINGHOUSE
1954 East Washington Avenue
Madison, Wisconsin 53704-5291

HOT LINES

800-COC-AINE

800-622-2255
National Council on Alcoholism—New York City

800-548-8700
Narcotics Education—Washington, D.C.

800-522-5353
Division of Substance Abuse Services, New York

800-554-KIDS
    554-5437
National Federation of Parents for Drug-Free Youth

800-ALC-ALLS
New York State Council on Alcoholism

APPENDIX 2: SUMMARY OF SOME

SUBSTANCE	COMMON OR SLANG NAMES	ACTIVE INGREDIENT
ALCOHOL	BOOZE, JUICE, SAUCE, BREW, VINO	ETHANOL, ETHYL ALCOHOL
MARIJUANA (CANNABIS)	POT, GRASS, DOPE, WEED, HOMEGROWN, SINSEMILLA, MAUI-WOWIE, THAI STICKS, JOINTS, ROACHES, INDICA, CONCEN-TRATED RESIN CALLED HASH OR HASHISH	TETRAHYDROCANNABI-NOLS (THC)
AMPHETAMINES	UPS, UPPERS, SPEED, CRANK, RX DIET PILLS	AMPHETAMINE, DEX-TROAMPHETAMINE, METHAMPHETAMINE (DESOXYEPHEDRINE)
NONPRESCRIPTION STIMULANTS	UPS, UPPERS	MAY CONTAIN CAF-FEINE, EPHEDRINE, PSEUDOEPHEDRINE, PHENYLPROPANOLAM-INE (PPA)
COCAINE	COKE, ROCK, TOOT, BLOW, SNOW, PEARL FLAKE	COCAINE, HYDRO-CHLORIDE (BENZOYL-METHYLECGONINE)
COCAINE, FREEBASE	BASE, FREEBASE, CRACK, ROCK	COCAINE BASE
BARBITURATES	BARBS, BLUEBIRDS, BLUES, TOOIES, YELLOW JACKETS	PHENOBARBITAL, PEN-TOBARBITAL, SECOBAR-BITAL, AMOBARBITAL
METHAQUALONE	LUDES, 714'S, SOPOR	METHAQUALONE
HEROIN	H, JUNK, SMACK, CHINA WHITE, BLACK TAR	DIACETYL, MORPHINE

SUBSTANCES USED FOR NONMEDICAL PURPOSES

SOURCE	PHARMACOLOGIC CLASSIFICATION	MEDICAL USE
NATURAL (FROM FRUITS, GRAINS, VEGETABLES)	CNS DEPRESSANT	SOLVENT, ANTISEPTIC, SEDATIVE
NATURAL (FROM CANNABIS SATIVA)	CNS DEPRESSANT, HALLUCINOGEN	ANTIEMETIC IN CANCER CHEMO-THERAPY
SYNTHETIC	CNS STIMULANT	CONTROL APPETITE, NARCOLEPSY—SOME CHILDHOOD BEHAV-IORAL DISORDERS, RELIEVE DEPRESSION
SYNTHETIC/NATURAL	CNS STIMULANT, DECONGESTANT, APPETITE DEPRESSANT	NONE
NATURAL (FROM COCA LEAVES)	LOCAL OR TOPICAL ANESTHESIA	LOCAL OR TOPICAL ANESTHESIA
NATURAL (PREPARED FROM COCAINE HYDROCHLORIDE)	LOCAL OR TOPICAL ANESTHESIA	TOPICAL ANESTHETIC OINTMENTS
SYNTHETIC	SEDATIVE HYPNOTIC	SEDATION EPILEPSY
SYNTHETIC	SEDATIVE HYPNOTIC	SEDATION
SEMI-SYNTHETIC (FROM MORPHINE)	NARCOTIC ANALGESIC	NONE LEGALLY

SUBSTANCE	COMMON OR SLANG NAMES	ACTIVE INGREDIENT
ANALOGS OF SYNTHETIC NARCOTICS	CHINA WHITE, SYNTHETIC HEROIN, MPTP, MPPP, PEPAP	ANALOGS OF SYNTHETIC NARCOTICS (FENTANYL, MEPERIDINE, PHENCYCLIDINE)
MORPHINE	WHITE STUFF, M, MORF	MORPHINE
CODEINE	SCHOOLBOY	METHYLMORPHINE
OXYCODONE		14-HYDROXYDIHYDRO-CODEINONE
MEPERIDINE		MEPERIDINE, HYDRO-CHLORIDE
METHADONE	DOLLY	METHADONE, HYDRO-CHLORIDE
INHALANTS	SOLVENTS, GLUE, TRANSMISSION FLUID, TYPEWRITER CORRECTION FLUID	ORGANIC SOLVENTS
NITROUS OXIDE	LAUGHING GAS, GAS, WHIPPITTS, NITROUS, BLUE BOTTLE	NITROUS OXIDE
BUTYL NITRITE	LIQUID INCENSE, ROOM DEODORIZER, RUSH, LOCKER ROOM, POPPERS	BUTYL NITRITE
LSD	ACID, LSD-25, BLOTTER ACID, WINDOWPANE, NAMED AFTER PICTURES ON PAPER, MESC	D-LYSERGIC ACID, DIETHYLAMIDE
MESCALINE (PEYOTE CACTUS)	MESC, PEYOTE, PEYOTE BUTTONS	MESCALINE

SOURCE	PHARMACOLOGIC CLASSIFICATION	MEDICAL USE
SYNTHETIC	NARCOTIC ANALGESIC	NONE
NATURAL (FROM OPIUM)	NARCOTIC ANALGESIC	PAIN RELIEF
NATURAL (FROM OPIUM), SEMI-SYNTHETIC (FROM MORPHINE)	NARCOTIC ANALGESIC	EASE PAIN & COUGH-ING
SEMI-SYNTHETIC (MORPHINELIKE)	NARCOTIC ANALGESIC	PAIN RELIEF
SYNTHETIC	NARCOTIC ANALGESIC	PAIN RELIEF, PREVENT WITHDRAWAL DISCOM-FORT
SYNTHETIC	NARCOTIC ANALGESIC	PAIN RELIEF, TREATMENT OF NARCOTIC ADDIC-TION
SYNTHETIC	NONE	NONE
SYNTHETIC	INHALATION ANESTHETIC	ANESTHESIA
SYNTHETIC	VASODILATOR	NONE (AMYL NITRITE USED IN ANGINA PECTORIS)
SEMI-SYNTHETIC (FROM ERGOT ALKALOIDS)	HALLUCINOGEN	EXPERIMENTAL RESEARCH ONLY
NATURAL (FROM PEYOTE CACTUS)	HALLUCINOGEN	NONE

SUBSTANCE	COMMON OR SLANG NAMES	ACTIVE INGREDIENT
MDA, MDE, MDMA, MMDA	LOVE DRUG, ECSTASY, XTC, ADAM	VARIOUS METHOXY-LATED AMPHETAMINES
PSILOCYBIN	MAGIC MUSHROOMS, SHROOMS	PSILOCYBIN
PCP	CRYSTAL, TEA, THC, ANGEL DUST	PHENCYCLIDINE
*COFFEE, TEA, COLAS	ESPRESSO, CAFE, NATURAL STIMULANT, GUAR-ANA, GUARANINE	CAFFEINE
TOBACCO	CIGS, SMOKES, BUTTS, CANCER STICKS, COFFIN NAILS	NICOTINE

*These substances have been included because of their potential habit-forming properties and widespread excessive use to the detriment of the health of the user.

Reprinted with the permission of:
Pharmaceutical Manufacturers Association
110 Fifteenth Street, N.W.
Washington, D.C. 20005

SOURCE	PHARMACOLOGIC CLASSIFICATION	MEDICAL USE
SYNTHETIC	AMPHETAMINE-BASED HALLUCINOGEN	NONE
NATURAL (FROM PSILO-CYBE FUNGUS, A TYPE OF MUSHROOM)	HALLUCINOGEN	NONE
SYNTHETIC	DISSOCIATIVE ANES-THETIC	ONCE USED AS A VET-ERINARY ANESTHETIC
NATURAL	CNS STIMULANT	MILD STIMULANT
NATURAL (FROM NICOTINIA TABACUM)	CNS TOXIN	EMETIC

SUBSTANCE	ABUSE FORM AND HOW USED	
ALCOHOL	LIQUID	TAKEN ORALLY, APPLIED TOPICALLY (RUBBING ALCOHOL)
MARIJUANA (CANNABIS)	PLANT PARTICLES (DARK GREEN OR BROWN)	SMOKED OR EATEN
AMPHETAMINES	TABLETS, CAPSULES, LIQUID, POWDER (WHITE)	TAKEN ORALLY OR INJECTED
NONPRESCRIPTION STIMULANTS	TABLETS OR CAPSULES	TAKEN ORALLY
COCAINE	POWDER (WHITE) OR LIQUID	SNORTED OR INJECTED
COCAINE, FREEBASE	WHITE CRYSTAL, SLIVERS RESEMBLING SOAP SHAVINGS	SMOKED (INHALED VAPORS)
BARBITURATES	TABLETS OR CAPSULES	TAKEN ORALLY OR INJECTED
METHAQUALONE	TABLETS	TAKEN ORALLY OR SNORTED

EFFECTS SOUGHT	LONG-TERM POSSIBLE EFFECTS	DEPENDENCE POTENTIAL	DETECTABLE IN URINE
INTOXICATION, SENSORY ALTERATION, ANXIETY REDUCTION	TOXIC PSYCHOSIS, NEUROLOGIC AND LIVER DAMAGE; FETAL ALCOHOL SYNDROME	YES	YES
EUPHORIA, RELAXATION, INCREASED PERCEPTION	BRONCHITIS, CONJUNCTIVITIS, POSSIBLE BIRTH DEFECTS	YES	YES
ALERTNESS, ACTIVENESS	LOSS OF APPETITE, DELUSIONS, HALLUCINATIONS, TOXIC PSYCHOSIS	YES	YES
ALERTNESS, ACTIVENESS, WEIGHT LOSS	HYPERTENSION, STROKE, HEART PROBLEMS	YES	YES
STIMULATION, EXCITATION, EUPHORIA (SUBTLE)	LOSS OF APPETITE, DEPRESSION, CONVULSIONS, NASAL PASSAGE INJURY, HEART ATTACK, STROKE, SEIZURE	YES	YES
INTENSIFIED COCAINE EFFECTS	WEIGHT LOSS, DEPRESSION, HYPERTENSION, HALLUCINATIONS, PSYCHOSIS, CHRONIC COUGH	YES	YES
ANXIETY REDUCTION, EUPHORIA	SEVERE WITHDRAWAL SYMPTOMS, POSSIBLE CONVULSIONS, TOXIC PSYCHOSIS	YES	YES
EUPHORIA, APHRODISIAC	COMA, CONVULSIONS	YES	YES

SUBSTANCE	ABUSE FORM AND HOW USED	
HEROIN	POWDER (WHITE, GRAY, BROWN)	INJECTED, SNORTED OR SMOKED
ANALOGS OF SYN-THETIC NARCOTICS	POWDERS	INJECTED OR SNORTED
MORPHINE	POWDER (WHITE), TABLETS OR LIQUID	TAKEN ORALLY OR INJECTED
CODEINE	TABLETS OR LIQUID (IN COUGH SYRUP)	TAKEN ORALLY OR INJECTED
OXYCODONE	TABLETS	TAKEN ORALLY OR INJECTED
MEPERIDINE	TABLETS OR LIQUID	TAKEN ORALLY OR INJECTED
METHADONE	TABLETS OR LIQUID	TAKEN ORALLY OR INJECTED
INHALANTS	VARIOUS	INHALED OR HUFFED (POURED ON A RAG OR TOWEL AND INHALED BY MOUTH)
NITROUS OXIDE	GAS IN PRESSURIZED CONTAINER	INHALED
BUTYL NITRITE	LIQUID	INHALED

EFFECTS SOUGHT	LONG-TERM POSSIBLE EFFECTS	DEPENDENCE POTENTIAL	DETECTABLE IN URINE
EUPHORIA	ADDICTION, CONSTIPATION, LOSS OF APPETITE	YES	YES
EUPHORIA	ADDICTION, MPTP INDUCED PARKINSONISM	YES	YES
EUPHORIA	ADDICTION, CONSTIPATION, LOSS OF APPETITE	YES	YES
EUPHORIA	ADDICTION, CONSTIPATION, LOSS OF APPETITE	YES	YES
EUPHORIA	ADDICTION, CONSTIPATION, LOSS OF APPETITE	YES	YES
EUPHORIA	ADDICTION, CONSTIPATION, LOSS OF APPETITE	YES	YES
EUPHORIA	ADDICTION, CONSTIPATION, LOSS OF APPETITE	YES	YES
INTOXICATION	IMPAIRED PERCEPTION, COORDINATION, JUDGMENT, TOXICITY FROM SOLVENT IMPURITIES	YES	RARELY TESTED FOR
EUPHORIA, RELAXATION	KIDNEY OR LIVER DAMAGE, PERIPHERAL NEUROPATHY, SPONTANEOUS ABORTION	POSSIBLE	NO
EXHILARATION	DAMAGE TO HEART AND BLOOD VESSELS, MAY AGGRAVATE HEART PROBLEMS	POSSIBLE	METHEMAGLOBIN IN BLOOD

SUBSTANCE	ABUSE FORM AND HOW USED	
LSD	TABLETS, CAPSULES, LIQUID, OR PAPER SQUARES	TAKEN ORALLY
MESCALINE (PEYOTE CACTUS)	TABLETS, CAPSULES, RAW DRUG (BUTTONS)	TAKEN ORALLY
MDA, MDE, MDMA, MMDA	TABLETS OR CAPSULES	TAKEN ORALLY
PSILOCYBIN	MUSHROOMS, RARELY AS TABLETS OR CAPSULES	TAKEN ORALLY
PCP	TABLETS, POWDER IN SMOKING MIXTURES	SMOKED, SNORTED OR TAKEN ORALLY
*COFFEE, TEA, COLAS	BEVERAGE	TAKEN ORALLY
TOBACCO	SNUFF, PIPE CUT PARTICLES, CIGARS OR CIGARETTES	SMOKED, SNORTED OR CHEWED

EFFECTS SOUGHT	LONG-TERM POSSIBLE EFFECTS	DEPEN-DENCE POTENTIAL	DETECTABLE IN URINE
INSIGHT, DISTORTION OF SENSES, EXHILARATION, MYSTICAL/RELIGIOUS EXPERIENCE	MAY INTENSIFY EXISTING PSYCHOSIS, PANIC REACTIONS	POSSIBLE	YES
SAME AS LSD	MILDER THAN LSD	POSSIBLE	NO
SAME AS LSD	NEUROTOXIC	POSSIBLE	YES
SAME AS LSD	MILDER THAN LSD	POSSIBLE	NO
DISTORTION OF SENSES	PSYCHOTIC BEHAVIOR, VIOLENT ACTS, PSYCHOSIS	YES	YES
ALERTNESS	MAY AGGRAVATE HEART PROBLEMS	YES	YES
RELAXATION	LOSS OF APPETITE, ADDICTIVE, LUNG CANCER, EFFECTS ON FETUS	YES	YES

INDEX

S

San Francisco (Calif.), 105, 135
Sauter, Diane, 10
Schuster, Charles, 13
Sedative-hypnotics, 158–163
Sheehan, John, 30
Sinsemilla, 130
Sleeping pills. *See* Barbiturates
Snappers. *See* Amyl nitrite
Speed. *See* Amphetamines
Stimulants, 152–155, 174, 180
  body's reaction, 152
  coffee and caffeine, 153–154
  dangers, 153
  reasons for use, 152–153
STP, 146
Strong, Robert, 2
Synthetic narcotics, 176, 182

T

THC (tetrahydrocannabinol), 128, 130, 133

Thompson, Veronica, 45
Tobacco, 178, 184
Tranquilizers, 162–163
Trowers, Reynolds, 10–11

U

Uppers. *See* Amphetamines

V

Velazquez, Felix, 44
Velez, Jane, 18

W

Walker, Ben, Jr., 22
Washton, Arnold, 7, 17–18, 25
Wine, 159
Women, 17–19

Y

Yage, 144–145
Youth at Risk program, 119–121

ABOUT THE AUTHOR

Dr. Essie E. Lee is a graduate of Columbia University and a professor of Community Health Education at Hunter College, New York. She has a background in health, guidance, and education, and has devoted many years to research, prevention and intervention strategies in the field of drug addiction. Dr. Lee has worked as a nurse, counselor and teacher, and serves on several boards, foundations and health service organizations. Her leisure activities include sports fishing, travel, and collecting Asian artifacts. She has written about a variety of topics, including health careers, alcohol, women, marriage and families, teenage depression, and the health sciences.